THE WONDERFUL ANIMATED WORLD OF

The WIZARD of OZ

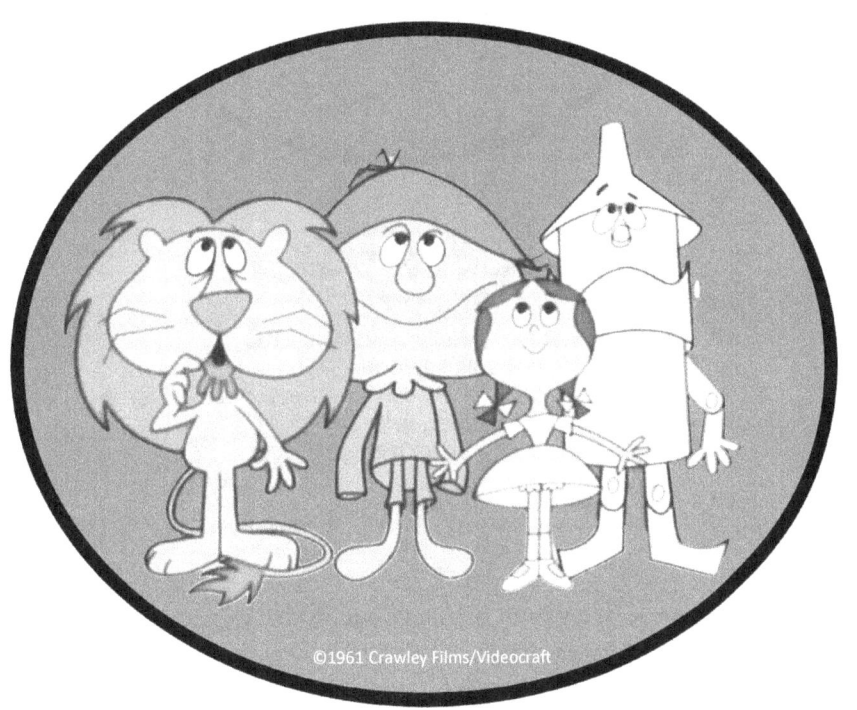

©1961 Crawley Films/Videocraft

By Kevin Scott Collier

THE WONDERFUL ANIMATED WORLD OF
The WIZARD of OZ

By Kevin Scott Collier

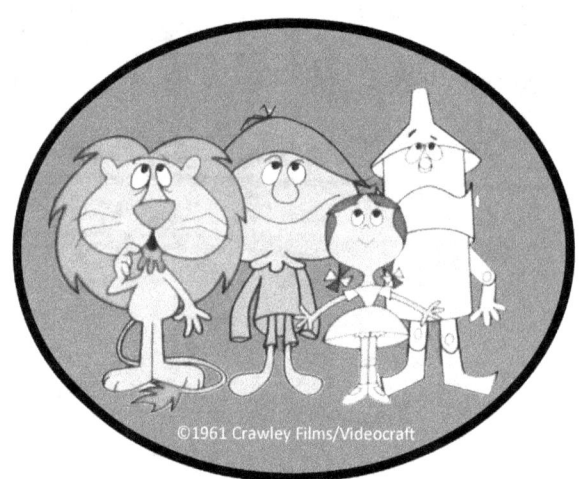

©1961 Crawley Films/Videocraft

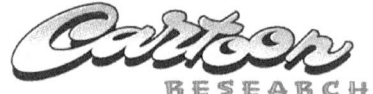

827 North Hollywood Way #100
Burbank, California 91505
Visit us online: www.cartoonresearch.com
Founder: Jerry Beck
Email: jerrybeck18@gmail.com

A special thanks to Jerry Beck, who provided select images for this book.

THE WONDERFUL ANIMATED WORLD OF THE WIZARD OF OZ, written as a historical document by Kevin Scott Collier. The images included in this book are © their respective copyright holders and are used as Fair Use to be illustrative for the text contained herein.

Sources: DVD and videos of the actual films and series, entertainment periodicals, promotional documents from productions, trade magazines, Library of Congress archives and misc. animation resources and historical Wizard of Oz and animation sites.

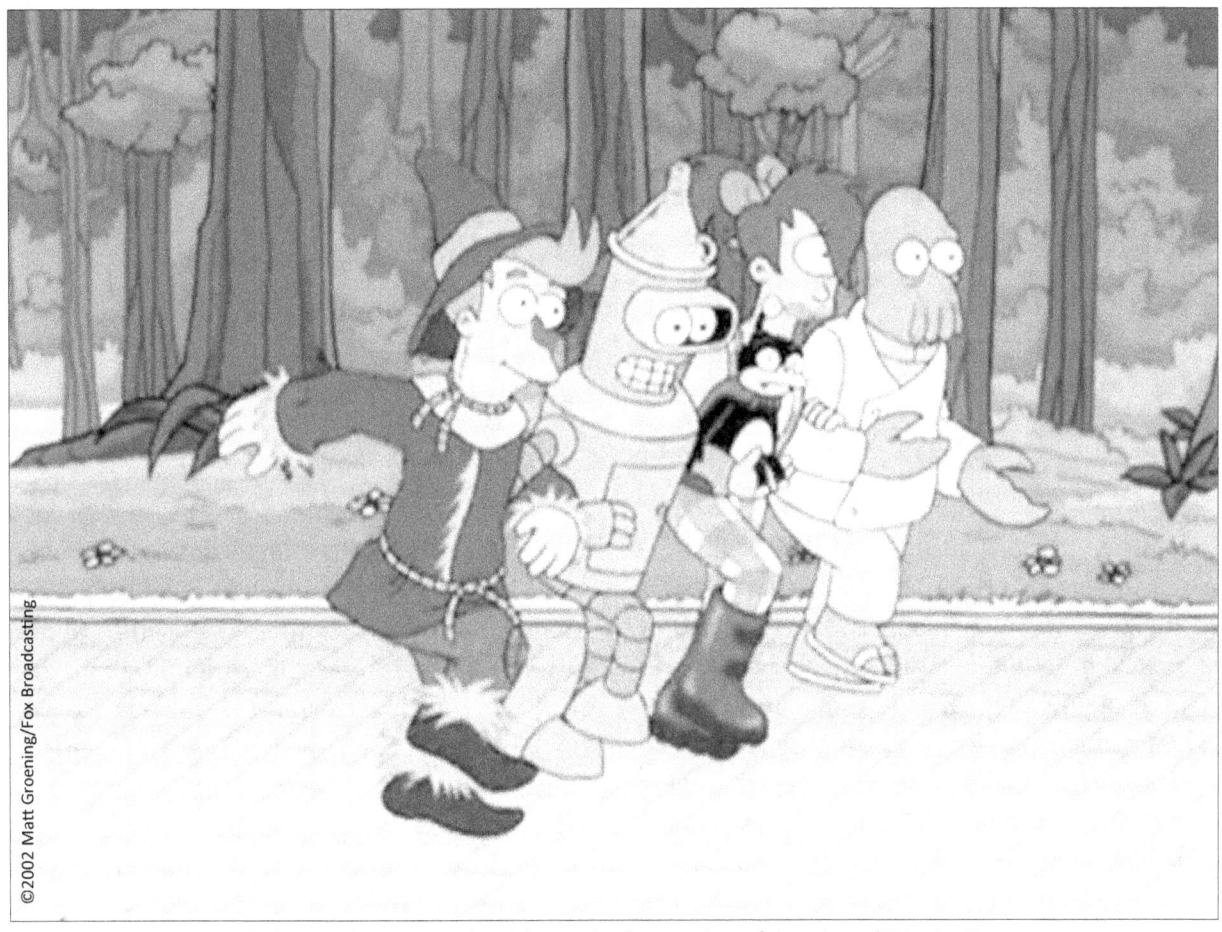

A *Wizard of Oz* parody appears in the 18th episode of season three of the animated TV series *Futurama*.

Lyman Frank Baum's Oz Animated

Lyman Frank Baum's book, *The Wonderful Wizard of Oz*, was published nearly 120 years ago. Little could the author have imagined the longevity of his characters, or where they would wind up in an advancing age of technology in the entertainment industry.

The world of Oz first appeared in animated cartoon form in 1933, but it wasn't until the 1960's that seemingly everyone wanted to jump on the bandwagon. Much of this was due to the fact that the original book had slipped into the public domain, and television networks, in succession, began broadcasting the original MGM classic as an annual TV special. While many of the noteworthy Oz animated adaptions of are detailed in this book, the theme also carried over into many cartoon television programs, movies, and specials.

In season four, episode eight of DC Comic's cartoon series *Super Friends*, the heroes were transformed into characters from Oz. The adventure, titled *The Planet of Oz*, was broadcast on November 10, 1979.

In the story, Mr. Mxyzptlk turns Superman, Aquaman, and Wonder Woman, into the Tin Man, the Scarecrow, and the Cowardly Lion, in that order.

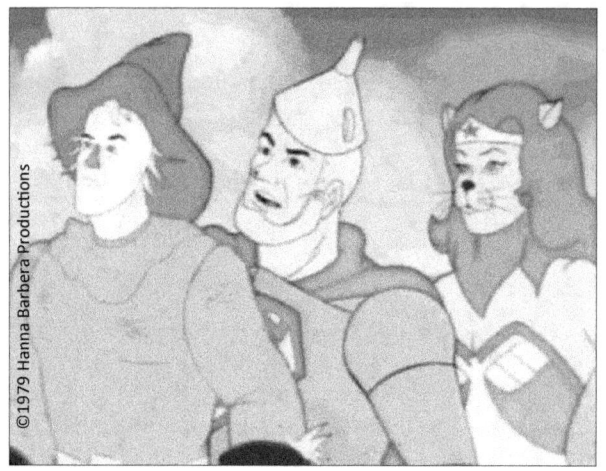

An Oz-themed episode of *Super Friends*, 1979.

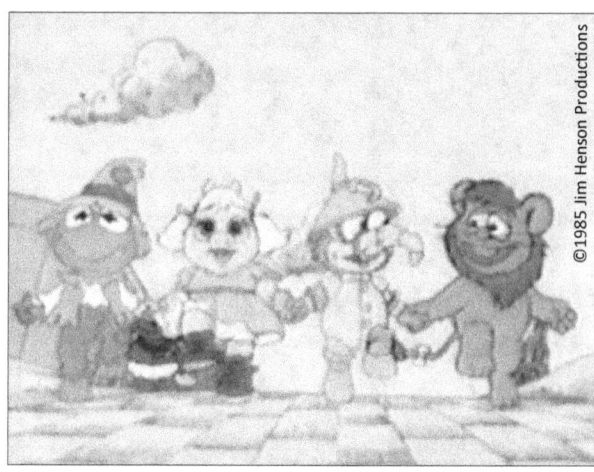

The *Muppet Babies* present an Oz episode, *1985*.

Batman escapes being part of Baum's fantasy, and stays at the Hall of Justice.

In season two, episode 12 of the cartoon series *Muppet Babies*, the kids play storytime and imagine they are part of the Oz tale. Their transformation and journey down the yellow brick road is cute, but Oz character design unremarkable. The show was broadcast November 30, 1985.

The 76th episode of the Warner Brothers cartoon series *Animaniacs, Buttons and Ows*, presented an Oz-based tale, broadcast on October 21, 1995.

In the third season, the 18th episode of *Futurama* featured an Oz parody. Titled *Anthology of Interest*, broadcast January 6, 2002, the cartoon series featured three imaginary stories, one being a take-off of the 1939 MGM film classic.

Subtitled *Wizzin'*, the segment presented Leela as Dorothy, with Bender as the Tin Man, Fry as the Scarecrow, and Zoidberg as the Cowardly Lion. Nibbler played Toto, and Professor Farnsworth became the Wizard.

In the parody, Dorothy wears a pair of oversized "magic boots."

The animated TV series *Family Guy* has presented many Oz moments.

According to Seth MacFarlane, they present the likenesses and characters from the Baum book series, as MGM refused to allow him to use anything that originated in the 1939 classic. However, in the episode *Herpe, the Love Sore*, which aired April 6, 2014, Dorothy is depicted wearing ruby slippers.

In the *Family Guy* episode *I Never Met the Dead Man*, broadcast April 11, 1999, the Wicked Witch of the West is featured.

Other Oz-related moments in *Family Guy* appear in the episodes *The Story on Page One, Holy Crap, Fast Times at Buddy Cianci Jr. High*, and a couple others.

The Simpsons cartoon has either mentioned Oz, or presented parodies of Baum's

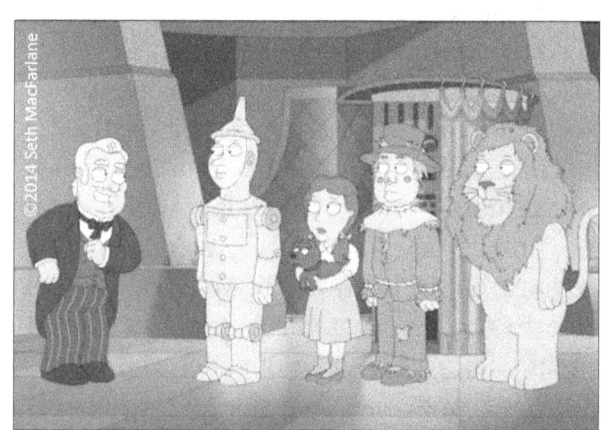

The series *Family Guy* has presented several Oz moments.

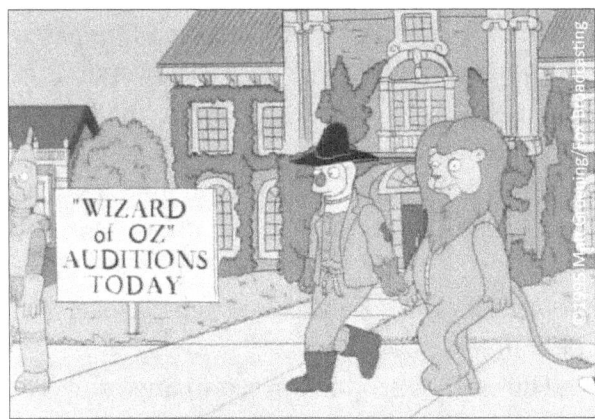

The Simpsons series has featured many Oz moments.

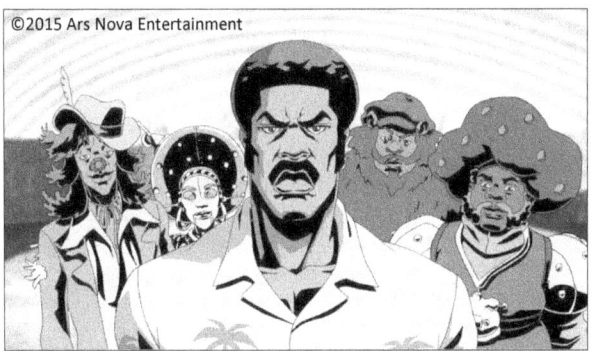

Black Dynamite in *The Wizard of Watts*, 2015.

characters, in 16 episodes during the series' run.

The most popular, *Lisa's Wedding*, from season six, episode 19, was broadcast March 19, 1995. In the tale, several Simpsons characters are dressed as the Tin Man, the Scarecrow, and the Cowardly Lion, auditioning for a *Wizard of Oz* play.

An episode of Nickelodeon's animated series *Rugrats* featured an Oz-based story, which was broadcast on October 2, 1999. In the story, Susie dreams she goes to *Lots of Tots Land*.

The cartoon *Phineas and Ferb* dove into the world of Oz in a two-part episode titled Wizard of Odd, broadcast September 24, 2010. In the story, Candace ends up in Patchkinland and meets the Wizard of Bustopolis.

On March 6, 2012, DIC and Cookie Jar Entertainment released a direct-to-DVD *Strawberry Shortcake* Oz tale titled *Berry Brick Road*. The 46-minute feature pretty much follows the 1900 Baum book.

The Disney Junior series *The Mickey Mouse Club* offered an Oz-themed episode with *Minnie's The Wizard of Dizz*, broadcast on September 13, 2013.

A 2015 episode of the animated series *Black Dynamite*, titled *The Wizard of Watts*, presented a hallucination Land of Oz tale for its streetwise, riotous cast.

The twisted Oz character cast included the Scarecorn, Lionhorn, Tin Bee, the Wicked B_tch, and the Great and Powerful Mother _____. You can fill in the blanks.

The Tom and Jerry animated features series of movies has presented Oz adventures, as well. *Tom and Jerry and The Wizard of Oz (2011)*, and *Tom and Jerry: Back to Oz (2016)*, both enjoyed commercial success on DVD.

Other feature films based on Baum's Oz include *Urfin Jus and His Wooden Soldiers*, also titled *Fantastic Journey to Oz*, produced by the CTB Film Company, released in Russia on April 20, 2017. An English language version does not exit. In the film, Dorothy is named Elly, who, with the Scarecrow, Tin

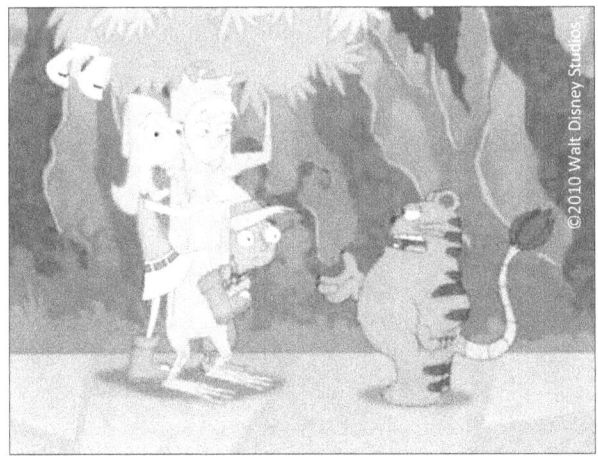

Phineas and Ferb follow the yellow brick road in 2010.

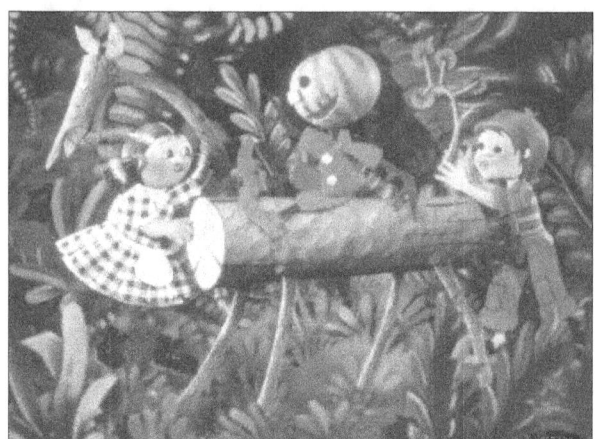

In the *Magical Land of Oz*, Polish stop-action TV series, 1983.

Man and Cowardly Lion, strive to defeat the wicked Urfin Jus, who seeks to rule all of Oz.

There are a few animated TV series about Oz that are not highlighted in this book's featured entries. One such show, *In the Magical Land of Oz*, was a stop-motion Polish animated series, was primarily based on Baum's books *The Wonderful Wizard of Oz*, *The Marvelous Land of Oz*, and *Dorothy and the Wizard of Oz*. The series made its debut in 1983, and ended in 1989. Only 13 episodes were produced.

Adventures in the Emerald City, a Russian animated four-part television series, released in 1999, provided some whimsical versions of Baum's Scarecrow and Tin Man characters, in particular. Never released in English, the series was primarily based on Baum's first and second Oz books. In the show, Dorothy was named Dolly, and is perhaps the ugliest depiction of the Kansas farm girl to ever appear in a cartoon.

The same production company also released a CGI animated, feature-length film, featuring the same character modeling.

Oz went Manga in 2007 with the animated cartoon series *Marchen Awakens Romance*. One-hundred and two episodes were produced. The series featured Dorothy Gale as a witch, Toto as a Rain Dog, the Crucified Scarecrow, Leo the Flying Lion, and Crazy Quilt, a take on the Patchwork Girl.

Oz themes have also contributed to countless television commercials in the past 50 years, selling everything from ravioli, to a public service announcement featuring the Tin Man's advice on how to keep a healthy heart.

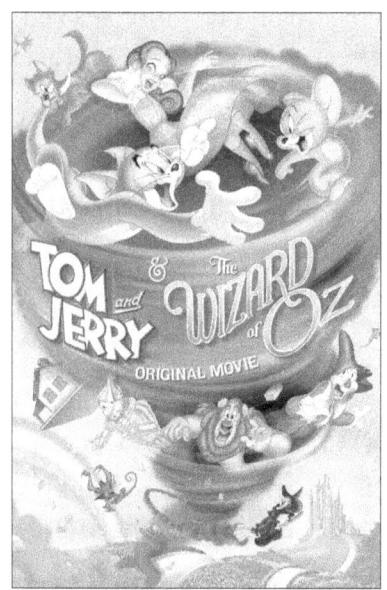 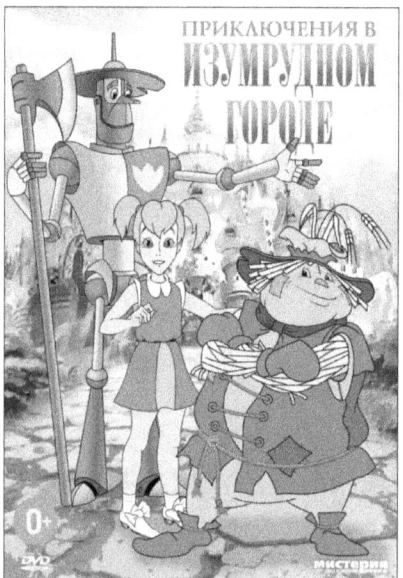 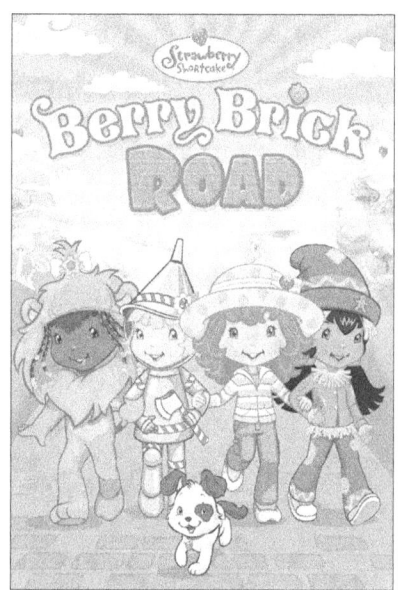

Warner Brothers' *Tom and Jerry and The Wizard of Oz*, Russia's *Adventures in the Emerald City* series, and *Strawberry Shortcake* in Oz.

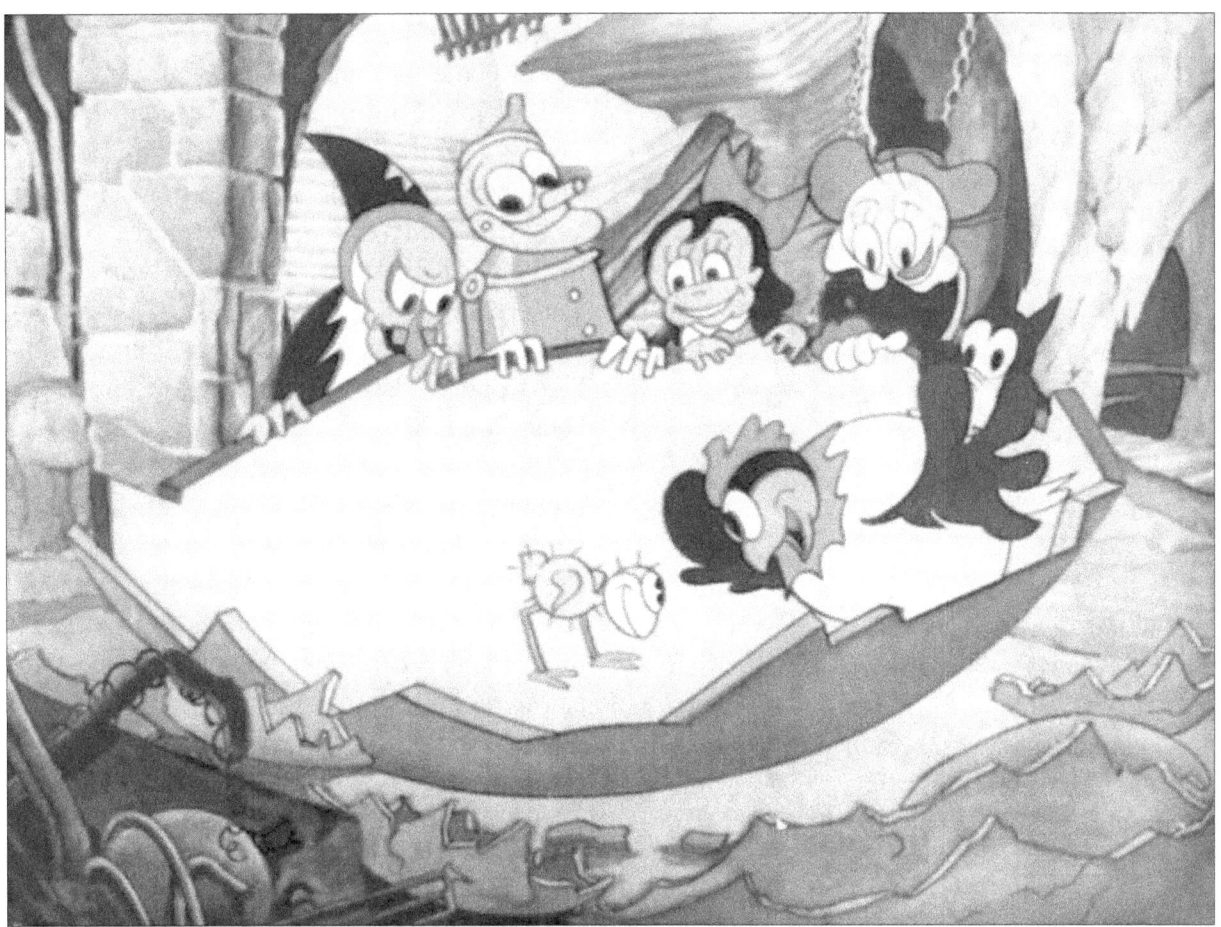

The final scene from *The Wizard of Oz*, released in 1933 by Ted Eshbaugh Studios.

The Wizard of Oz (1933)

The first animated cartoon produced and released based on Lyman Frank Baum's book, *The Wonderful Wizard of Oz*, was *The Wizard of Oz*, in 1933.

The short film, which runs eight and a half minutes, was produced by Ted Eshbaugh. Eshbaugh, an animated filmmaker, produced two cartoon shorts prior to *The Wizard of Oz*, *Goofy Goat Antics* (1930) and *The Snowman* (1931). His film production company, Ted Eshbaugh Studios, headquartered in New York, was operational for nearly 30 years.

One rare aspect of Eshbaugh's *The Wizard of Oz* at the time was it was filmed entirely in color. Color film was a new technology, rarely seen by the public at the time, and undoubtedly unaffordable for animation.

The Technicolor process seen in the cartoon was made possible with the use of the film laboratories of Canada.

The story featured in Eshbaugh's *The Wizard of Oz* is credited to Frank Joslyn Baum, the eldest son of *The Wonderful Wizard of Oz* author and creator, Lyman Frank Baum. His writing credit for the film appears as Col. Frank Baum. He was a Lieutenant Colonel in the United States Army.

How much Frank Joslyn Baum contributed

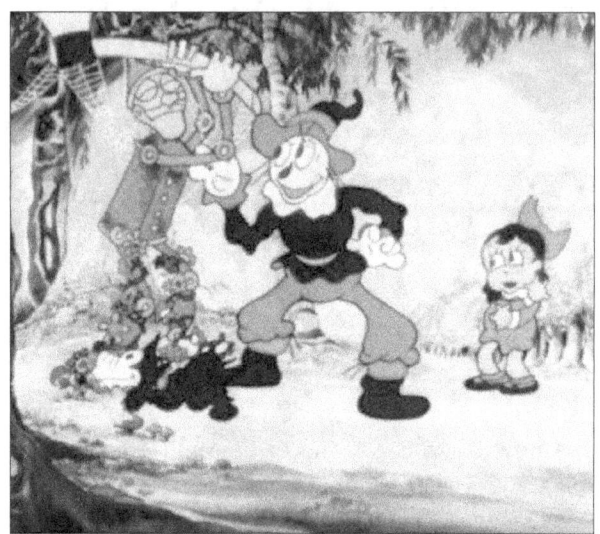

Dorothy, Toto and the Scarecrow meet the Tin Man in a scene from *The Wizard of Oz*, 1933.

Jesse "Vet" Anderson was a newspaper cartoonist and art instructor who previously worked in the animation departments of Paul Terry's Fables Studio, Barr Studios, and Fleischer Studios. It was reported in June 1933 that Anderson was admitted to a home for disabled veterans, and *The Wizard of Oz* was his final cartoon work. Andrew Hutchinson previously was an animator for Sherwood Wadsworth Pictures, Inc., and Red Head Comedies.

The film debuts a technique seen in the theatrical movie *The Wizard of Oz*, released six years later, which starred Judy Garland. The opening of the cartoon begins in black and white on the grey Kansas prairie, then turns to color after Dorothy is swept away in a cyclone to the land of Oz.

The film's story, absent the Cowardly Lion, presents Dorothy and Toto with companions The Scarecrow and the Tin Man. Several other characters emerge, including a creature likely based on the A-B-Sea Serpent featured in Ruth Plumly Thompson's *The Royal Book of Oz*, published in 1921.

The film tale begins when a tornado bears down on the Kansas plains, lifting Dorothy's home skyward. She, and her dog, Toto, tum-

to the story in the film has been a subject of debate. The tale is loosely based on his father's book. It is known he was involved in the production of the cartoon and profited off the project from the Oz lease arrangement with Eshbaugh.

> **Eschbaugh To Produce Color Cartoon Series**
>
> Ted Eschbaugh has organized his own company for the production of two series of color cartoons, "The Wizard of Oz," and "Color Fantasies." He has already finished the first of the Oz series, and is now making the initial Fantasy.
>
> Eschbaugh will do nothing on releasing until he can show at least one of each of the two series

Hollywood Reporter, January 16, 1933.

Frank Joslyn Baum, a lawyer, and writer, was also the very first president of *The International Wizard of Oz* club.

The cartoon, which doesn't feature much dialogue, presented classical music arrangements by Carl W. Stalling.

Illustrators on the project were Frank Tipper, Bill Mason, Cal Dalton, Vet Anderson and Andrew "Hutch" Hutchinson.

Tipper subsequently worked in the animation departments of Warner Brothers and Walter Lantz Studios. Mason went on to work as an animator for Disney. Dalton joined the animation department at Warner Brothers, also.

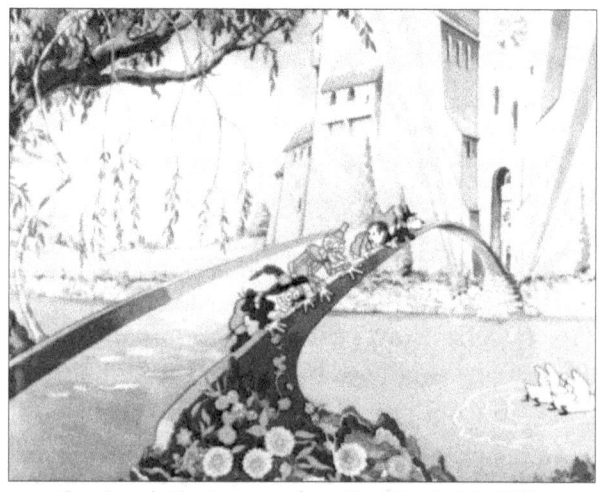

Crossing a bridge in a scene from *The Wizard of Oz*, 1933.

ble out down to terra firm, landing in a cornfield. There she meets The Scarecrow. Freeing him from his pole, the three journey forward.

Along the way, they encounter the frozen, rusted Tin Man. The Scarecrow produces a can of oil to bring the metal man back to mobility. Brushed off and cleaned up, he joins along on the journey.

The four see many colorful creatures leading to the city of Oz, such as butterflies, swans, and peacocks. They arrive at the Emerald City and are given a welcoming reception complete with a parade. Dorothy and her companions ride in a coach.

One scene features suits of armor, no one inside, providing a song, *Hail to the Wizard of Oz! To the Wizard of Oz, we lead the way!*

They meet with the Wizard, who appears to be a sinister-looking, but relatively harmless character. He sports a white-beard, and a wears a black robe covered with stars, along with a conical hat. He performs several magic tricks for their enjoyment.

In one scene, a chicken lays a number of eggs, but what hatches from them are anything but chicks. When a subsequent egg laid

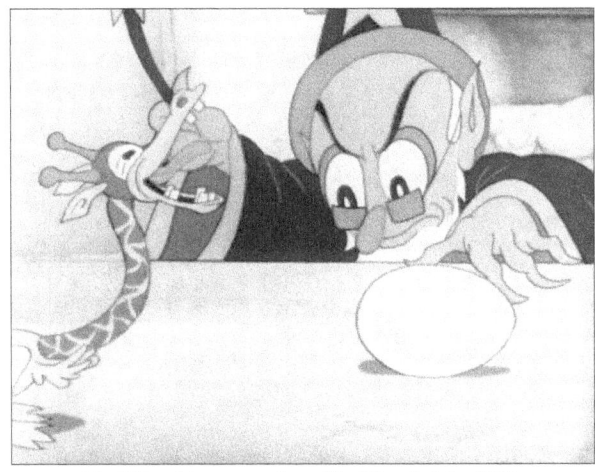

The Wizard, in a scene from *The Wizard of Oz*, 1933.

grows to an enormous size, the foursome becomes alarmed. The Tin Man cracks the egg open, and a tiny chick emerges. The mother hen joins her newborn as the song *Rock-a-bye Baby* plays, concluding the cartoon.

Ted Eshbaugh got into trouble with the Technicolor Corporation before the film's release. Eshbaugh had made the movie without the proper licensing agreement with Technicolor. The 3-strip color process, which was expressly used by Disney, resulted in a lawsuit that didn't allow *The Wizard of Oz* to be released in color. Thus, prints of the film were issued in black and white only.

Over the past decades, the film has been available in its original color format for viewing and purchase. Eshbaugh's Oz cartoon has appeared for commercial sale on Betamax tape, VHS, Laserdisc, CED, and DVD.

A restored print of the color film is included in the 2005 3-Disc Collector's Edition of the more famous 1939 MGM live-action feature film.

Thunderbean Animation restored and remastered the film for a 2014 Blu-ray and DVD as compilation *Technicolor Dreams and Black and White Nightmares*. The transfer is stunning and worth owning.

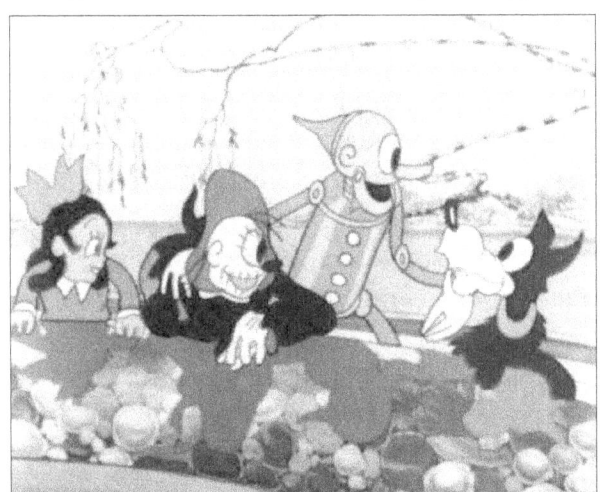

Dorothy, the Scarecrow, the Tin Man, and Toto float on a log in the water in a scene from *The Wizard of Oz*, 1933.

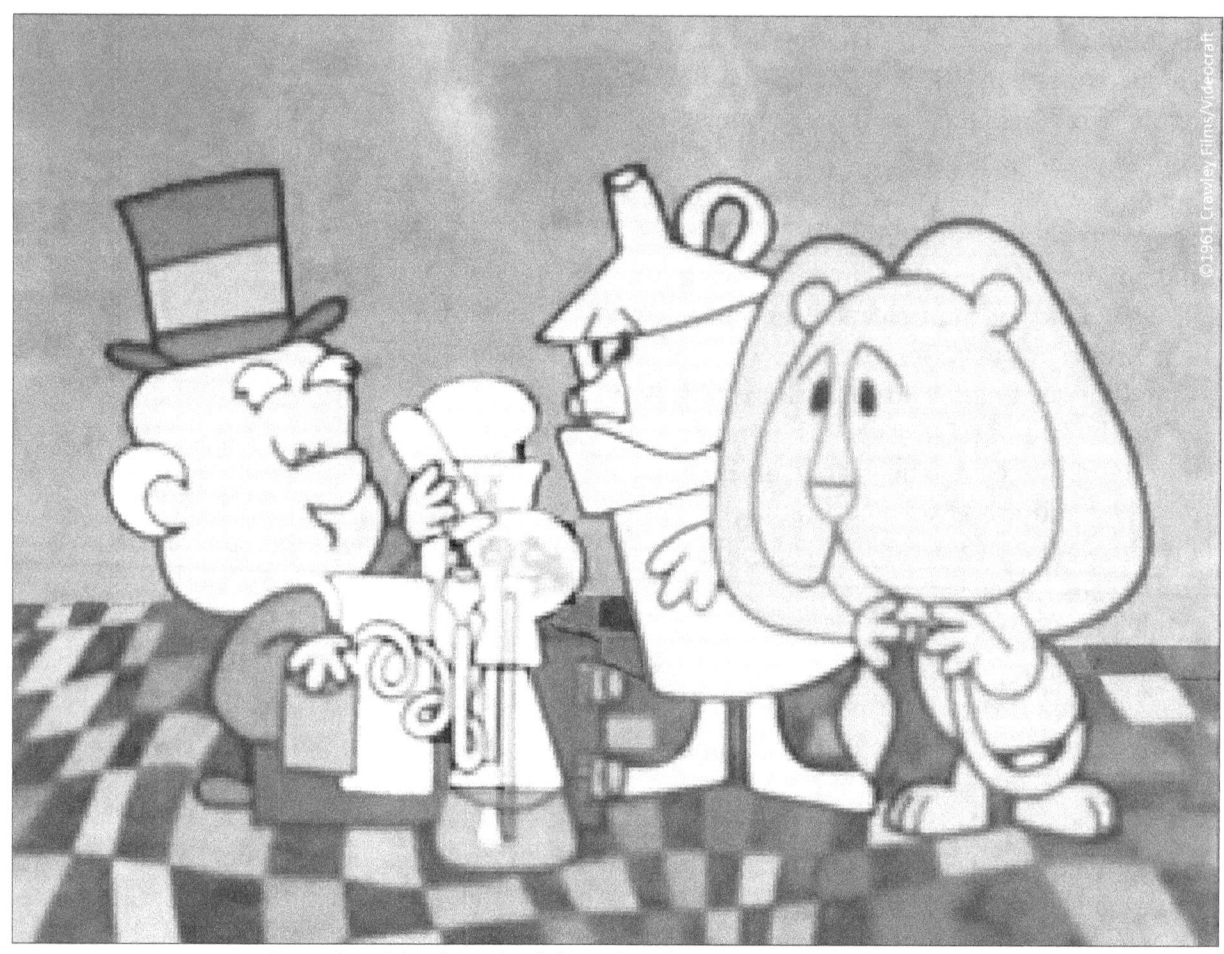

A scene from *Tales of the Wizard of Oz*, released in 1961, Crawley Films/Videocraft.

Tales of the Wizard of Oz (1961)

The second animated adaptation of Lyman Frank Baum's book, *The Wonderful Wizard of Oz*, was *Tales of the Wizard of Oz*, a made-for-television series that made its debut on the NBC network September 1, 1961.

The color program originated from Crawley Films, for Videocraft, which subsequently became Rankin/Bass Productions. Crawley films was founded by Frank Radford Crawley in 1939.

The series, comprised of 130 five-minute adventures, was produced by Arthur Rankin Jr., Jules Bass, Larry Roemer, Antony Peters, and Bernard Cowan. Harry Kerwin directed.

Crawley Films, operating out of Ottawa, sold the series in a package that also included *The New Adventures of Pinocchio*. *Broadcasting* magazine stated, "it is believed that this is the first large-scale animated cartoon series to be produced out of Canada."

Vic Atkinson served as the supervising animator, with Frank Crawley's wife, Judith, heading the script department.

English and French language versions of the series were released.

Lyman Frank Baum characters were given additional names in the series, such as Dandy the Cowardly Lion, Rusty the Tin Man and

Socrates the Scarecrow.

Five talents provided the voices for the primary characters. Dorothy was played by Corrinne Conley, Dandy Lion and The Wizard was voiced by Carl Banas, Larry D. Mann performed Rusty the Tin Man, Socrates the Scarecrow was played by Alfie Scopp, and Peggi Loder was both Good Witch Glinda and The Wicked Witch of the West.

Peggy Morse primarily provided voices for the Munchkins. Performing the voices for guest and secondary characters were Bernard Cowan, Stan Francis, Susan Morse, and James Doohan.

Carl Banas provided voices for many animated cartoon series during his long career, including *King Kong*, *Spider-Man*, and *Babar*.

TV Cartoon Series In Production At Ottawa
Crawley Making Wizard Of Oz
By JACK MARSTERS, Television Editor of The Gazette

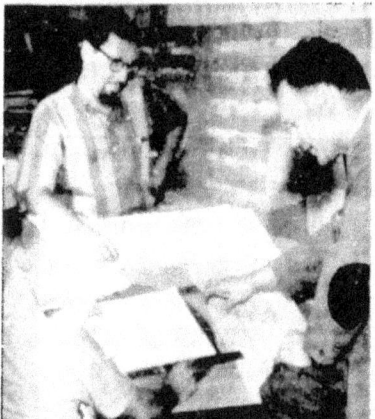

Cartoon conference between Bill Mason, continuity supervisor, Tony Peters, art director of Videocraft, and Tom Glynn, Crawley producer.

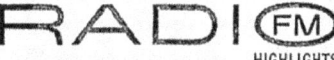

Dorothy, Toto and the Scarecrow meet the Tin Man in a scene from *The Wizard of Oz*, 1933.

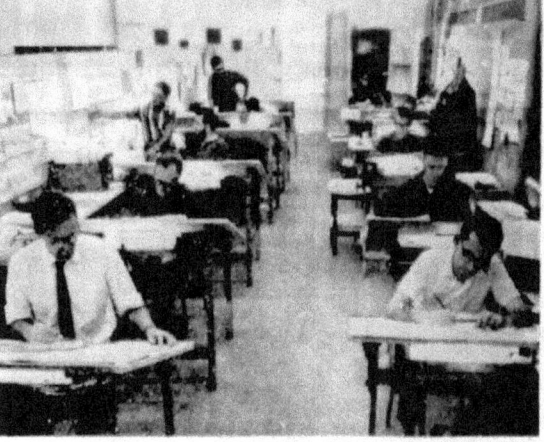

Animators drawing the main action of the Wizard of Oz cartoons

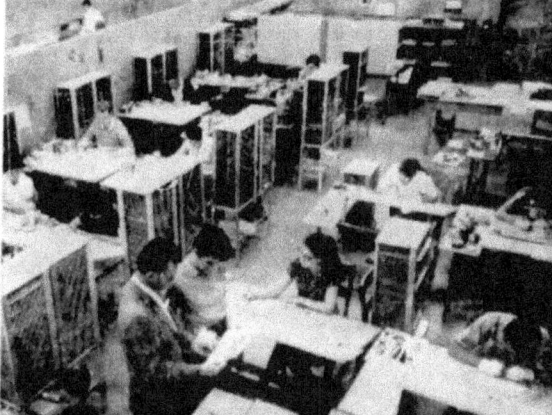

Tracing and painting section of the cartoon department at Crawley Films

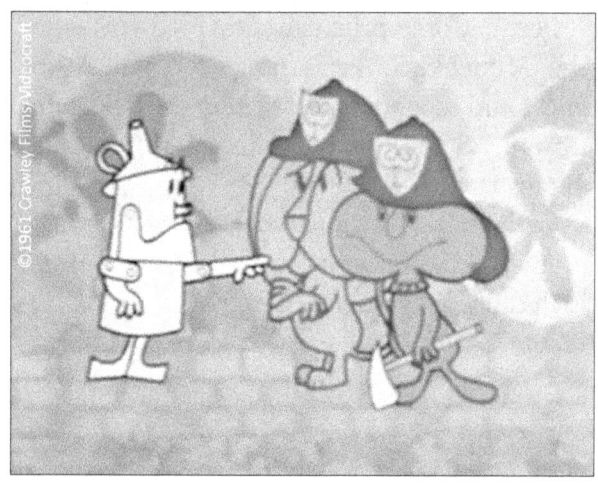

From *Tales from the Wizard of Oz, Fire Chief* episode.

Corrinne Conley was an actress, who during her career, appeared in TV shows such as *Hogan's Heroes, That Girl, Sanford and Son* and *Quincy, M.E.*

Larry Mann was an accomplished actor who in his early years appeared as Cap'n Scuttlebutt and Flub-A-Dub on the *Howdy Doody Show*. His acting credits included such programs as *My Favorite Martian, Voyage to the Bottom of the Sea, The Green Hornet* and *Bewitched*. He was the voice of Yukon Cornelius in Rankin/Bass' 1964 production of *Rudolph the Red-Nosed Reindeer*.

Peggi Loder and Alfie Scopp both played bit parts in TV shows like *The Wayne and Shuster Show* and *Encounter*. Scopp also did voices for the TV cartoons *King Kong*, and *Spider-Man*, among others.

Susan Morse was an actress and voice artist best known for her subsequent works in *Adventures in Rainbow County*, and *The Forest Rangers*. She also did the voice of Susan bond for the *King Kong* cartoon.

James Doohan, who lent his voice to a handful of episodes, is most recognized for his role as the chief engineer of the starship Enterprise, Montgomery "Scotty" Scott, in the classic *Star Trek* television series.

Examples of episodes present a simple, yet curious tales, which usually involve a mystery with a solution at the conclusion. Many of the episodes didn't feature the entire cast equally but highlighted one or two on an adventure. Fewer numbers provided for some character development. Also, the logistics of trying to cram Dorothy, the dog, her three companions, the Wizard, an evil witch, good witch and piles of Munchkins into one episode was impossible.

In the episode, *The Golden Touch*, Rusty the Tin Man dreams that everything he touches turns to gold. But the Midas touch isn't all it's cracked up to be, as food and necessities turn to gold with a tap, rendering them useless. When Glinda sends Socrates the Scarecrow to deliver a heart to Rusty, he can't touch that, either. He awakes, and his fortune remains relegated to a nightmare.

In the episode *One Big Headache*, Socrates the Scarecrow visits the Wizard to improve his smarts. The Wizard removes his head and departs to catch some fish, "brain food," to help. During his absence, the scarecrow wanders off, but in parts. His head and body are found, and the search is on to reunite the two.

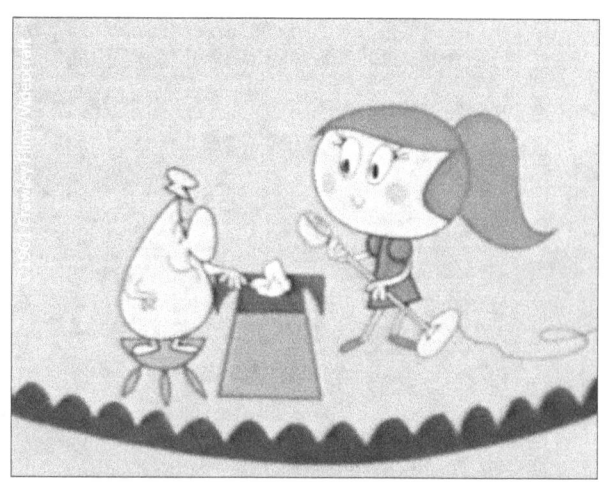

From *Tales from the Wizard of Oz, The Raffle* episode.

An advertisement for *Tales of the Wizard of Oz* series.

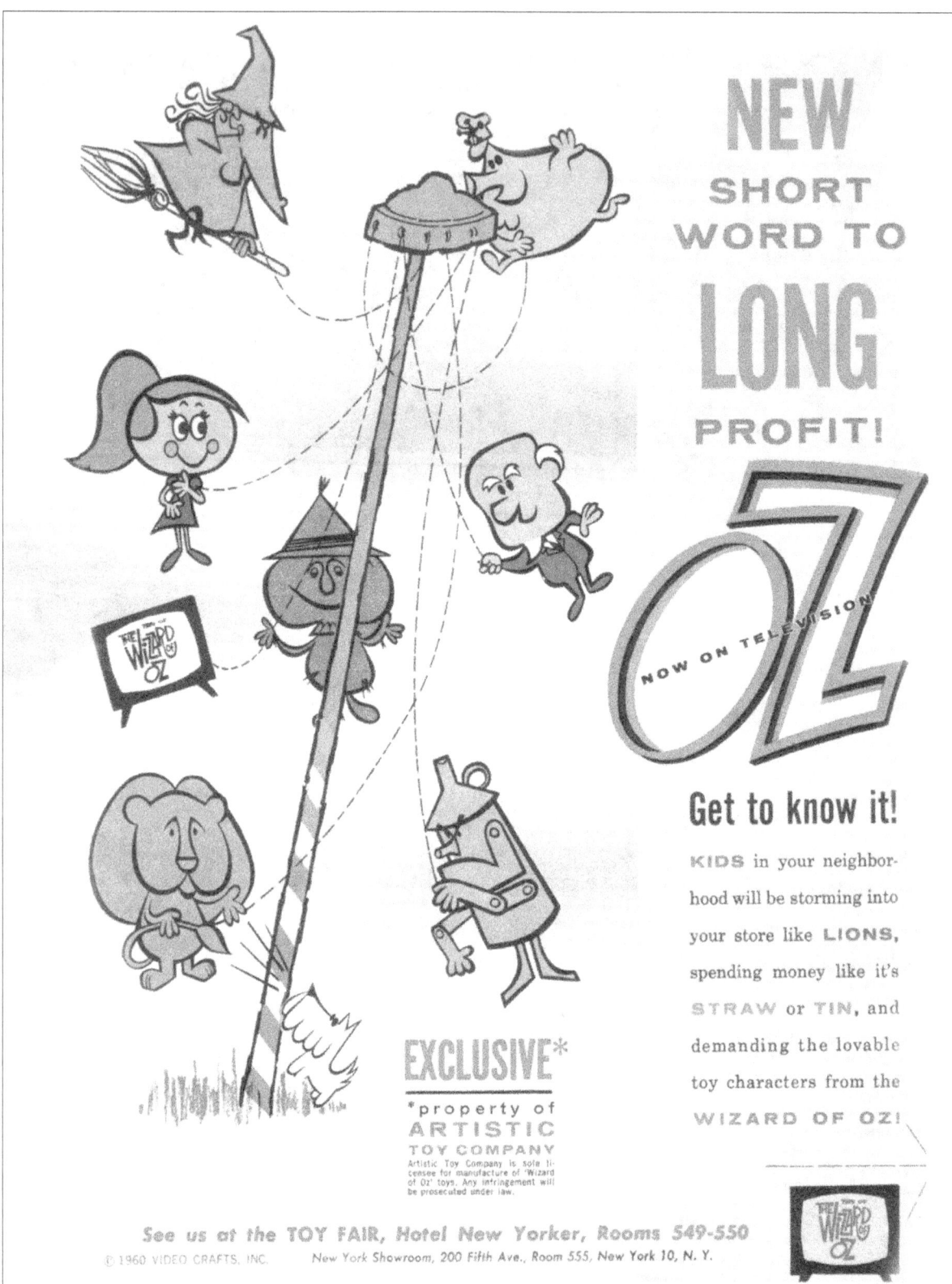

An advertisement for *Tales of the Wizard of Oz* series.

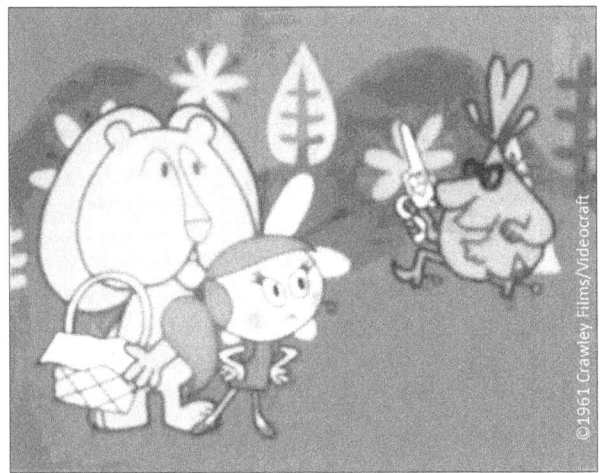

From *Tales from the Wizard of Oz*, Munchkin Robin Hood episode.

In the episode *Well Done*, the Wicked Witch of the West strikes a deal with the Desmond the Dragon sending him on a mission to eat Dorothy. The dragon arrives at a cookout for Dorothy hosted by Dandy the Lion. But, the gentle and timid dragon is reluctant to fulfill his mission. So he is invited to the picnic.

In the episode, *The Skills of Bravery*, Dandy the Lion is frightened of Desmond the Dragon when the creature suffers from a case of the hiccups. Rusty tries to teach Dandy about bravery with training lessons in self-defense.

In the episode, *The Sucker*, Dandy the Lion becomes frightened during a nighttime stroll. While scared of his own shadow, the ghost of his Grandfather appears. The spirit conjures up memories of Dandy as a child producing examples of early bravery facing dangerous creatures. The spirit suggests Dandy suck his thumb to restore his courage.

In the episode *Dinner Party*, Dorothy invites Dandy, Rusty, and Socrates over to her home for dinner. But Dorothy's cooking leaves much to be desired. She burns everything she cooks to serve. Her guest eats, without criticizing a thing, and depart with tummy aches.

In the episode *The Long Hair Dandy*, the Lion is obsessed with his beautiful hair. When Rusty musses up his mane, Dandy gets ruffled. Meanwhile, having a bad hair day herself, the Wicked Witch confronts Rusty and asks him to find her a wig. Rusty makes amends with Dandy and convinces the lion that like Sampson if his hair is cut off, he will become brave and strong. Rusty gathers up the hair providing the Witch with a wig.

In *Don't Pick the Daisies*, the Wizard uses his sizeable electronic computer to produce a heart for Rusty the Tin Man but hands him a bouquet of flowers instead.

In the episode *The Hillies and the Billies*, Dorothy tags along with the Wizard to do some mountain climbing. They chance upon a cabin occupied by Hillbillies. The mountain men are feuding with their neighbors and Dorothy, and the Wizard tries to make peace between the factions.

In the episode *The Gusher*, Rusty buys a plot of land from a wealthy Southern businessman that is supposed to harbor oil below. Rusty imagines a prosperous life with all its perks and signs the deed to a worthless piece of land. But luck is in his favor, as the

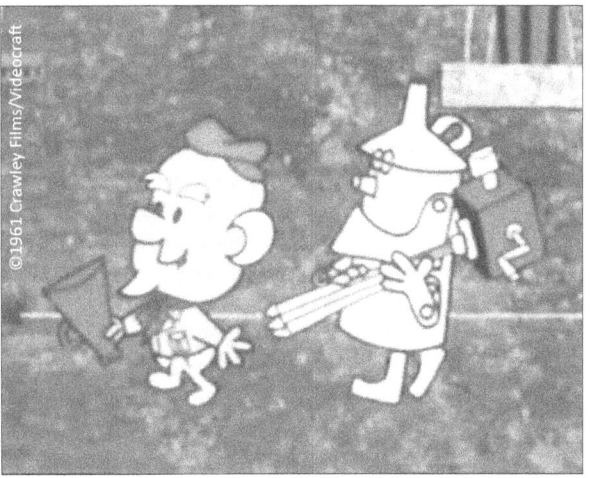

From *Tales from the Wizard of Oz*, Witch's Boyfriend episode.

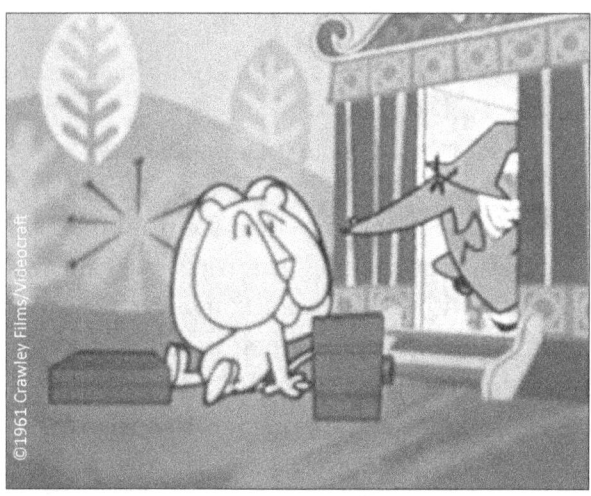

From *Tales from the Wizard of Oz, Family Tree* episode.

well strikes oil.

In *The Raffle*, Rusty, Socrates, and Dandy go sledding in winter. Dorothy approaches them asking them to buy a holiday raffle ticket. Rusty refuses until he discovers the grand prize is a heart. He buys all of the lottery tickets. The old ticker turns out to be made of ice and melts.

All of the episodes are simple-minded, yet amusing. There's not a lot of room for character development, but the antics of the wicked witch, and sometimes the misguided actions of the Wizard, propel Dorothy and her companions into a variety of unusual situations moving the pace of the action.

An unofficial DVD of *Tales of the Wizard of Oz* series was released. Episodes appear online for viewing. In 2010, the series began occasionally broadcast on the Retro Television Network.

Tales of the Wizard of Oz Episode Guide

Pilot: Part 1 / Pilot: Part 2 The Witch Switch / Leapin' Lion / The Magic Hat / The Balloon Buzz / Machine-Gun Morris / Movie Maid / Shadow Snakes / The Big Cake Bake / Desmond's Dilemma / Misfire Miss / Gung-Ho Gang / Heart Burn / Stuffed / The Fountain of Youth / The Rubber Man / The Happy Forest / Dandy's Dilemma / The Search / The Bag of Wind / The Music Men / To Bee or Not to Bee / Have your Pie and Eat it Too / The Sound of Munchkins / The Count / Places, Please / The Green Golfer / The Flying Carpet / The Monkey Convention / The Big Shot / On the Wing / To Stretch a Point / The Flipped Lid / Down in the Mouth / The Gusher / The Family Tree / Boomer Rang / The Great Laurso / The Pudgy Lion / Beauty and the Beach / The Hillies and Billies / The School Marm / An Optical Delusion / Watch the Bouncing Ball / All in a Lather / The Green Thumb / Leap Frog / The Cultured Lion / Chowy Mein / The Super-Duper Market / Friends of a Feather / Monkey Air Lift / Guaranteed for Life / The Skills of Bravery / The Coat of Arms / Roar, Lion, Roar / Be a Card / The Inferior Decorator / The Salesman / The Cat's Meow / The Yellow Brick Road / Rusty Rusty / The Scarecrow / The Invisible Man / Free Trade / The Bull Fighter / The Golden Touch / The Long Hair / Roll the Presses / The Big Brother / The Cool Lion / Gabe the Gobbler / The Raffle / The Strawman Twist / The Dinner Party / The Fire Chief / The Green Tomato / The Poet / The Three Musketeers / One Big Headache / Get Out the Vote / The Wizard's Promise / Well Done / The Do-It-Yourself Heart / The Great Auto Race / The Jail Breakers / The Reunion / The Sucker / The Bubble Champ / Too Much Heart / The Witch's Boyfriend / The Clock Watchers / Double Trouble / The O.N. / Going to Pieces / Mail-Order Lover / Love Sick / It's a Dog's Life / The Fallen Star / Don't Pick the Daisies / The Munchkin Robin Hood / The Wizard's Tail-Fins / The Rubber Doll / Return to Oz / To Stretch a Point / Down in the Mouth / The Gusher / The Family Tree / Boomer Rang.

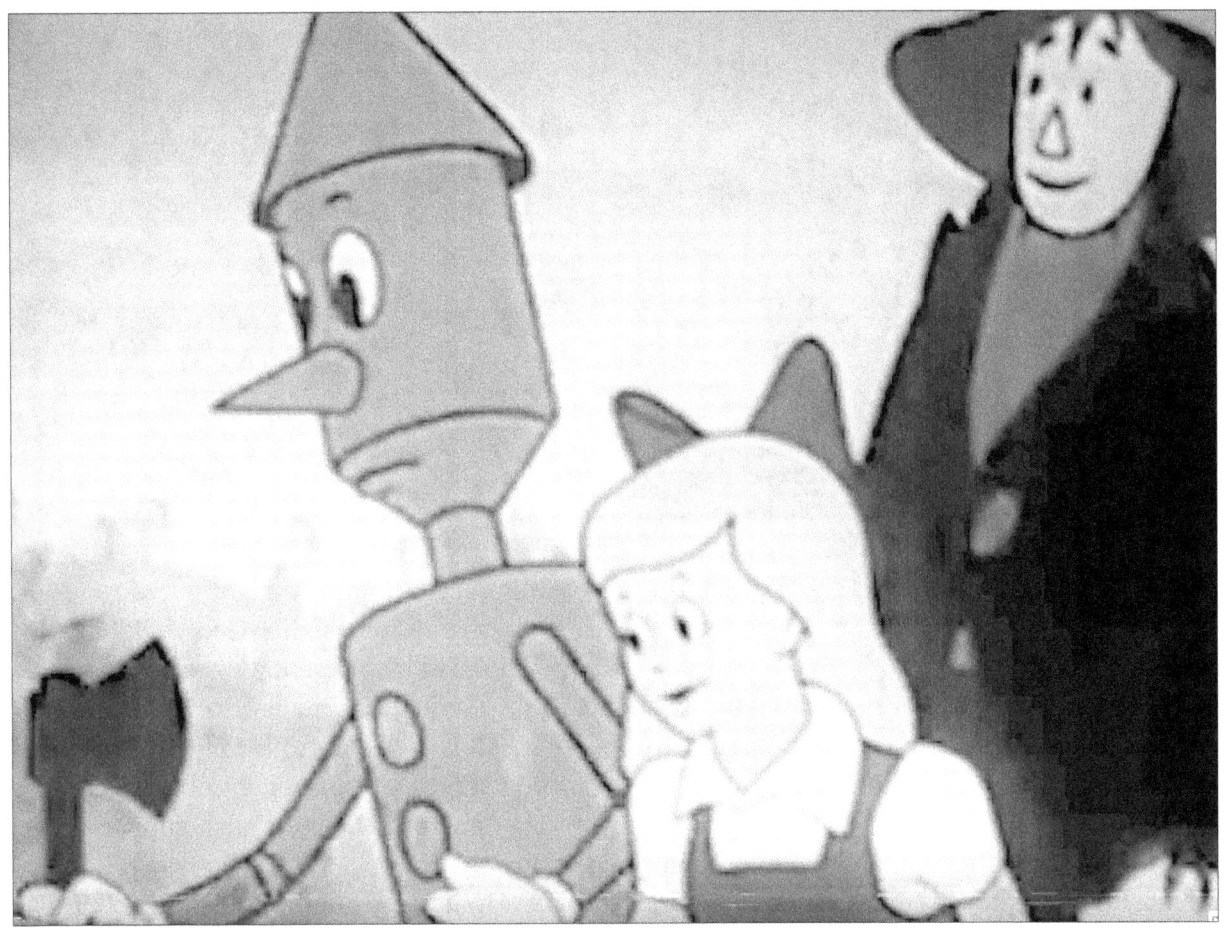

The Tin Man, Dorothy, and the Scarecrow, in a scene from *The Magic of Oz*, released in 1963 by Cartoon Film Presentations.

The Magic of Oz (1963)

The Magic of Oz, a Cartoon Film Presentation, was released in 1963. The nearly six-minute cartoon, a fragmented adaptation of Lyman Frank Baum's book, is best known for being unknown and also being called, "the worst cartoon ever."

George Litchfield produced the cartoon. Robert Capeheart directed, designed and animated the film. The story was written by Art Newman, with the script by Richfield and Quigley. Dave Hollister provided the voice of the Wizard and Lion. Raphael Remy served as director of photography. Paul Csonka composed the musical score.

The artistic style of *The Magic of Oz* resembles old Fleischer Studios cartoons. The opening image in the cartoon presents the head of the Wizard. He resembles a sultan, wearing a turban and earrings. Next, we see Dorothy, the Tin Man and the Scarecrow walking on the yellow brick road. They spot the Cowardly Lion and hide behind some brush to observe him. The king of the forest then breaks out into song.

The melody is interrupted when the lion is bitten on the tail by a snake slithering down a tree. The agitated lion then sees the Tin Man and Scarecrow. He punches the Tin Man,

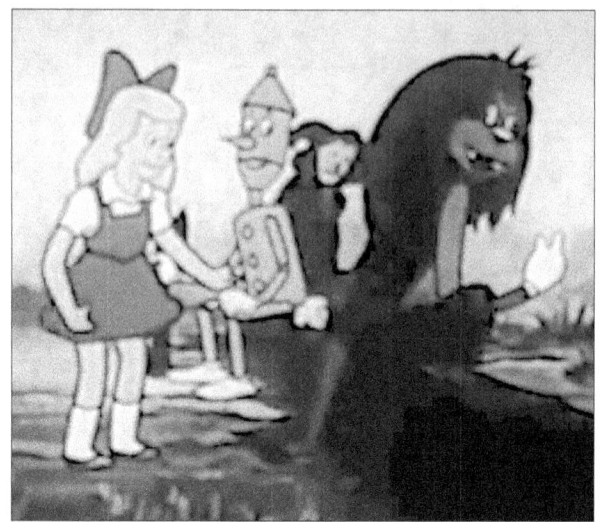 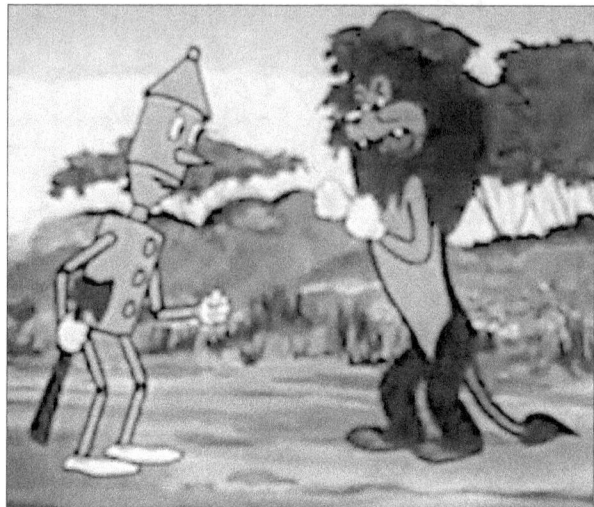

Dorothy, the Tin Man, the Scarecrow and the Cowardly Lion, in scenes from *The Magic of Oz*, 1963.

sending him to the ground, and knocks the stuffing out of the Scarecrow. Dorothy admonishes the beast.

Discovering the lion is a coward, the trio invites him to join them on their journey to Oz. Perhaps the Wizard can give him some courage.

Dorothy then breaks out in song, singing the wonders of the Wizard of Oz. The others join in, and continue down the yellow brick road headed for the Emerald City.

While the background illustrations display detail, the character artwork is simple without style. The animation is limited and weak, and scenes often repeated. Animators used some rotoscoping for depictions of Dorothy. The process involved using live models to build illustrations over.

Artistically, the lion is the only character that has a sweet appearance. Dorothy is incredibly creepy looking, and the Tin Man and Scarecrow are stiff and odd. Dorothy's dog Toto is absent from the film.

Perhaps the most creepy character is the Wizard, who is presented as a sultan with earrings and lipstick. The image appears at the beginning of the film, and is enough to leave small children with nightmares.

The assumption is this George Litchfield production was a presentation piece to sell a cartoon series or made-for-TV animated movie. It is evident from viewing that the cartoon represents a segment of a larger story. The length of the film also supports the notion.

The Magic of Oz enjoys no praise, but attracts curiosity due to its sheer creepiness. The animated short is so bad Cartoon Research founder Jerry Beck included it in his *Worst Cartoons Ever* show.

The film appears on YouTube.

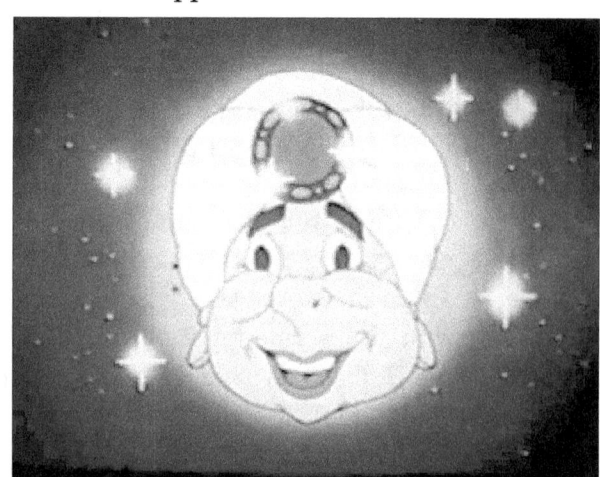

The Wizard, in a scene from *The Magic of Oz*, 1963.

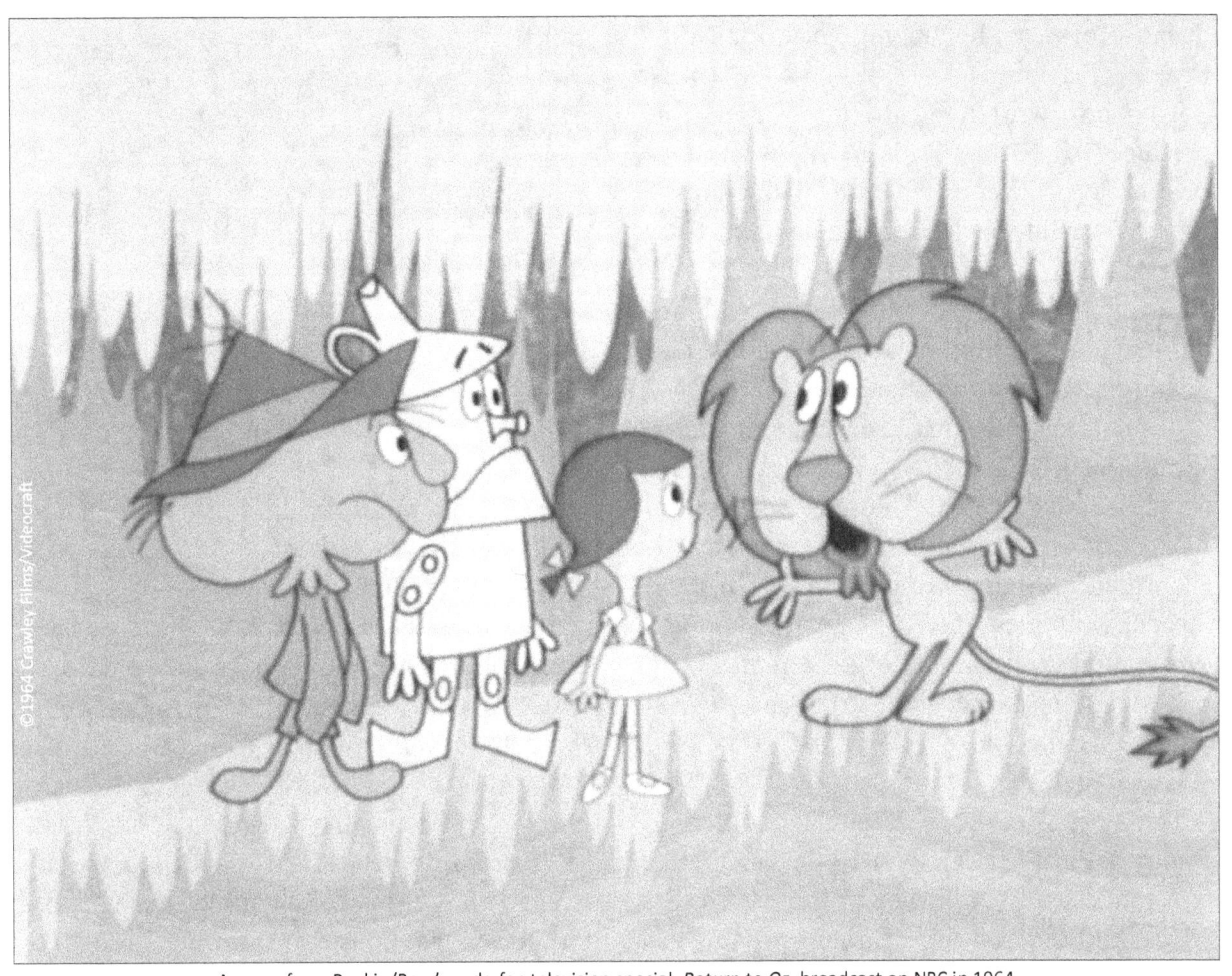

A scene from Rankin/Bass' made-for-television special, *Return to Oz*, broadcast on NBC in 1964.

Return to Oz (1964)

Return to Oz, produced by Crawley Films for Rankin/Bass (Videocraft) Productions, was a made-for-television animated special that first aired on the NBC network February 9, 1964. The feature, sponsored by General Electric, through Maxon, Inc., was based on Crawley Films' 1961 animated TV series, *Tales of the Wizard of Oz*. It featured the identical set of main characters, with slight artistic modifications and modeling.

Return to Oz originally ran 90 minutes in length, but was cut back to 51 minutes to fit a one-hour time slot. It made its debut as a part of *General Electric's Color Fantasy Hour* program.

The main characters included Dorothy, Dandy Lion, Rusty the Tin Man, Socrates the Scarecrow, The Wizard, Glinda, the Wicked Witch of the West, and Toto.

Back also was virtually the same team that took part in the television series.

The voices for the characters included Susan Conway as Dorothy, Carl Banas as Dandy and the Wizard, Peggi Loder as Glinda, Larry D. Mann as Rusty and Wicked Witch, Alfie Scopp as Socrates, Stan Francis as Toto, and

Susan Morse as the singing voice for Dorothy.

The film, written by Romeo Muller, was produced by Arthur Rankin, Jr., with Jules Bass as co-producer. In charge of cinematography was Bill Clark, Ron Haines and Gary Morgan. Music was written by Gene Forrell, James Polack and Edward Thomas, with additional composition by George Wilkins, and Edward Thomas as conductor.

Animators and their assistants included Vic Atkinson, Norman Drew, Margaret Falconer, Ginny Fripp, George Germanetti, Blake James, Bill Mason, Barrie Nelson, Michael Pacey, George Rufle, Ron Smith, Don Stearn, Milton Stein, Terry Tarricone, Jack White, Rod Willis, and George Cannata.

Among the background artists were Bob Borg, Patrick Coulson, George Germanetti, and Dennis Pike.

The story is basically a retelling of Lyman Frank Baum's first Oz book. But the special was marketed as a sequel to the TV series, which had entered syndication and still retained popularity with tykes. Merchandising of the series remained successful, too, thus the new entry would continue the momentum. An aim was also to bring the studio fur-

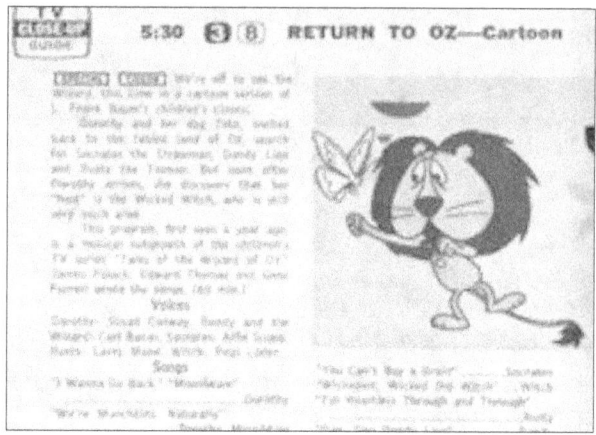
A TV Guide listing for *Return to Oz*.

ther acclaim, amid pending projects, such as *Rudolph the Red-Nosed Reindeer*, with songs sung by Burl Ives.

Return to Oz doesn't rekindle scenarios from the TV show, but does do something that the series failed to do—provide some character development for the cast.

The story opens with letters to Dorothy sent by her friends in Oz, who miss her greatly. It prompts her return. This time she arrives in Oz courtesy of an apple tree, not in a tornado-blown house.

Glinda greets Dorothy in Munchkin Land and presents her with the news that the previously melted Wicked Witch of the West has been resurrected. She is terrorizing the Land

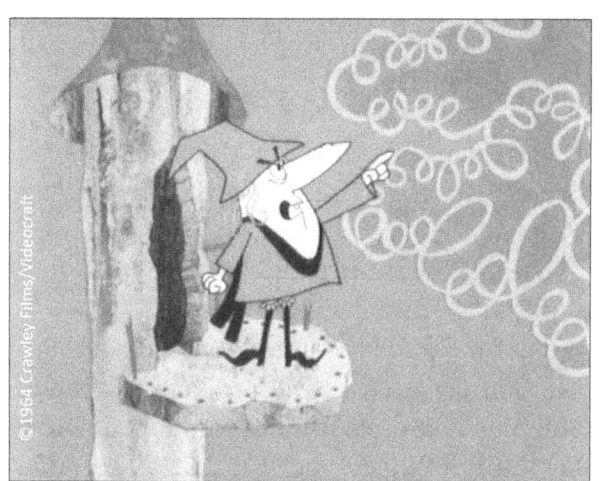
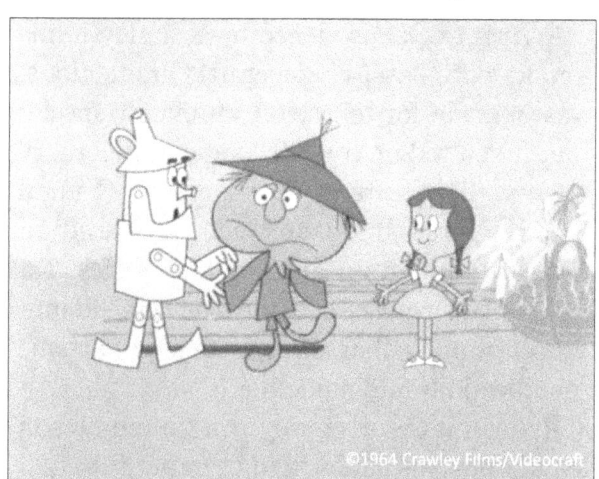
Scenes from Rankin/Bass' *Return to Oz*, which made its debut on NBC TV February 9, 1964.

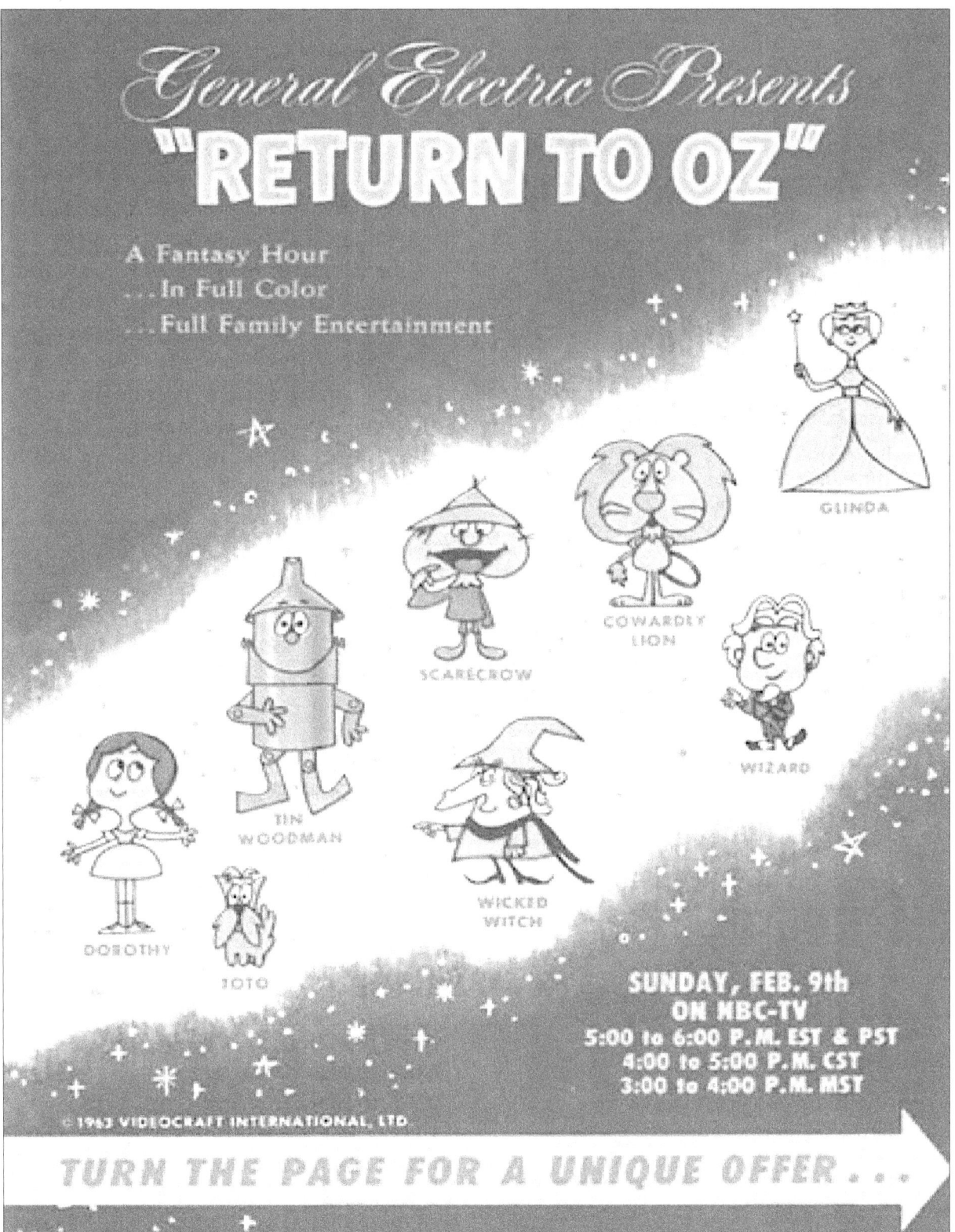

An advertisement for Rankin/Bass' Return to Oz, 1964.

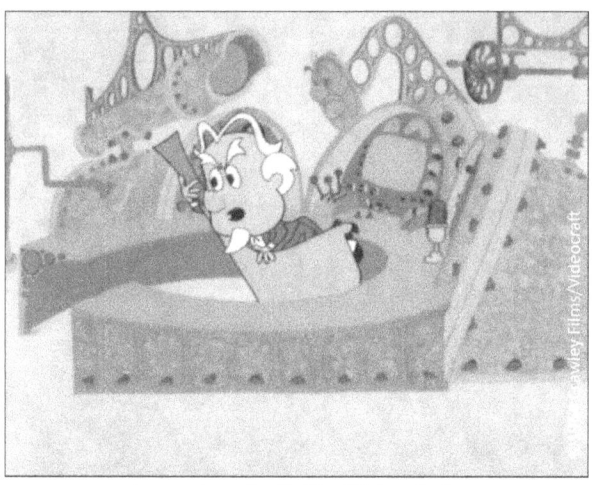

A scene from Rankin/Bass' *Return to Oz*.

of Oz. In her quest to be reunited with her friends, Dorothy discovers that the evil witch has burned Socrates' diploma, wrecked Rusty's heart, and stolen the medal of courage Dandy had worn proudly.

Her mission is now to restore what the Wizard had once given them.

Reunited, the gang head to the Emerald City. There they discover the evil witch has captured the Wizard's throne and appointed herself ruler of the kingdom. The Wizard himself requires restoration. He promises the group if they can defeat the witch, and restore him to power, he will reward everyone with what she had taken from them.

During the drama, Rusty is killed by a bolt of lightning while under attack, but is brought back to life by Glinda.

Some amusing additions include flying alligators who are at the witch's beck and call. Also, there's the Wizard's physical participation, joining the others at the witch's castle to assist in freeing Dorothy. Apparently, he got bored hiding behind a curtain.

At the end, it all works out, and evil is dealt a resounding defeat. The Witch, due to the backfire of her own curse, is turned to stone and crumbles. The Wizard hands out trinkets to satisfy what is emotionally missing in the Scarecrow, Lion, and Tin Man, but we know they never really lost intelligence, bravery or the ability to love.

The Wizard is unable to transport Dorothy home, as he has no true powers. Glinda steps in to make it happen.

She uses her magic to whip up a tornado that safely returns Dorothy and Toto back to their Kansas farmhouse.

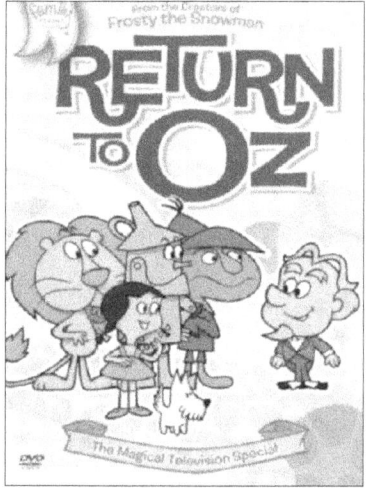

Return to Oz DVD, 2006.

In the 1980's, Prism Entertainment put *Return to Oz* out in VHS format.

Sony Wonder and Classic Media subsequently released the feature on DVD in March, 2006.

Return to Oz was played by local TV stations for several decades through syndication arrangements. A number from the film, *I Wanna Go Back*, sung by Susan Morse, became a popular tune among juveniles.

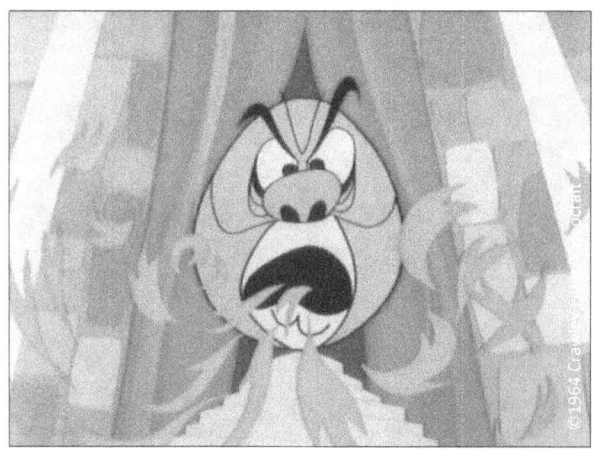

A scene from Rankin/Bass' *Return to Oz*.

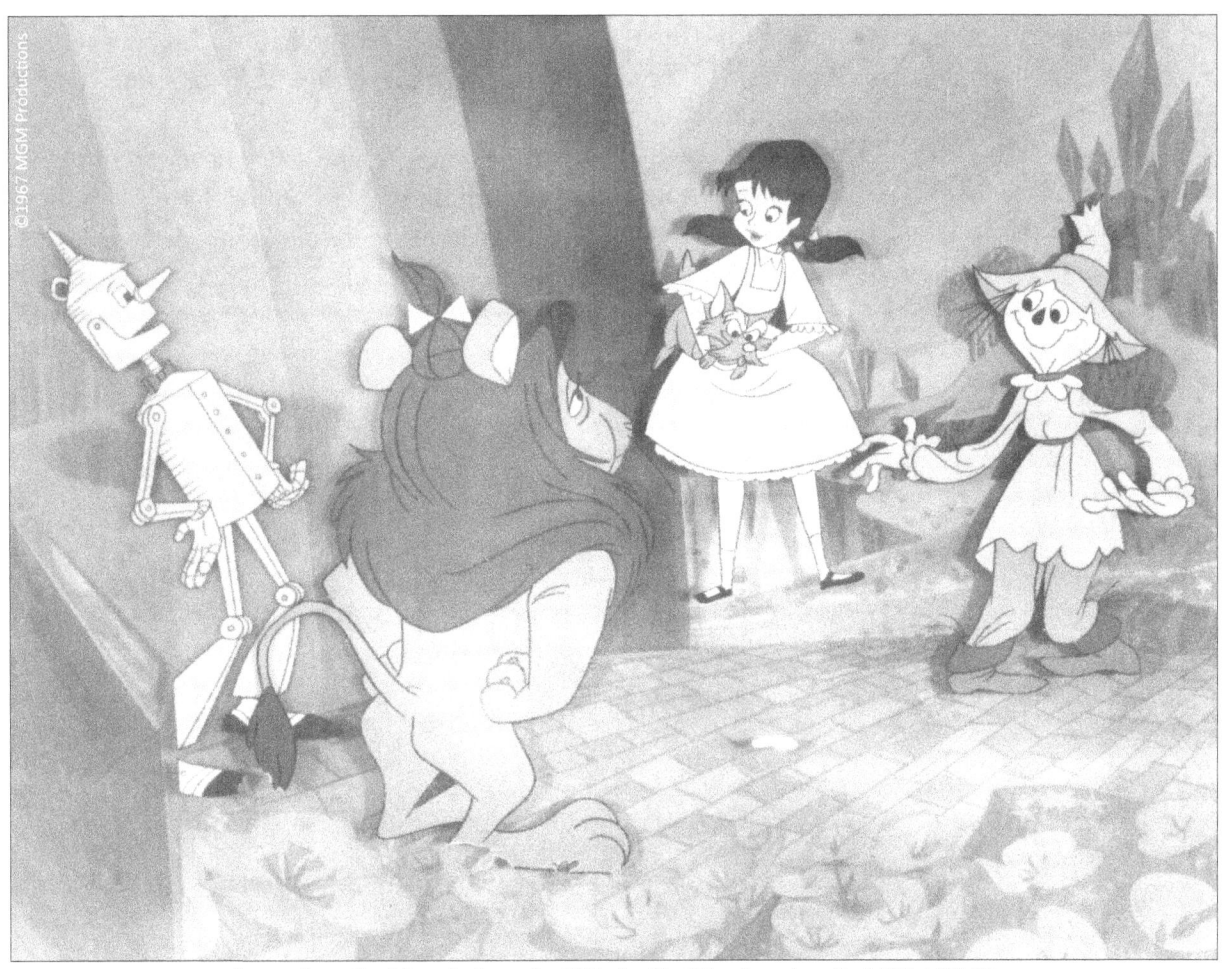

A scene from Chuck Jones' take on Oz, *Off To See The Wizard*, produced by MGM, 1967-68.

Off To See The Wizard (1967)

Perhaps the finest, most stylistic depictions of Lyman Frank Baum's characters in cartoon form appears in *Off To See The Wizard*, produced by MGM's Animation/Visual Arts Division, under the supervision of legendary animator, Chuck Jones.

The title may assume the television show was an Oz cartoon series, but the animated segments appeared at the beginning and end as a wraparound presenting a live-action, family-oriented film. ABC broadcast the program from September 8, 1967, to September 20, 1968.

MGM's Animation/Visual Arts Division, established in 1964, introduced *Off To See The Wizard* as an answer to *Walt Disney's Wonderful World of Color*, which presented family films and held a prime Sunday evening slot. The Division, headed by Jones, included general manager Les Goldman, chief design director Maurice Noble, and director Abe Levitow.

The short animated Oz segments were sometimes mini-stories, but routinely served as humorous introductions for the live-action films presented. The concept also was based on the 1939 MGM film starring Judy Garland, not Baum's book, *The Wonderful Wizard of Oz*. For the most part, characters were designed to resemble their live-action counterparts, such as the Lion resembling Bert Lahr, and The Wizard in the likeness of Frank Morgan. The show also included music that originated in the MGM classic, such as *Somewhere Over the Rainbow* and *We're Off to See The Wizard*.

While Jones' vision of Oz never spun off as a fully animated cartoon for Saturday morning television, merchandising of the Chuck Jones depictions of the characters was wildly

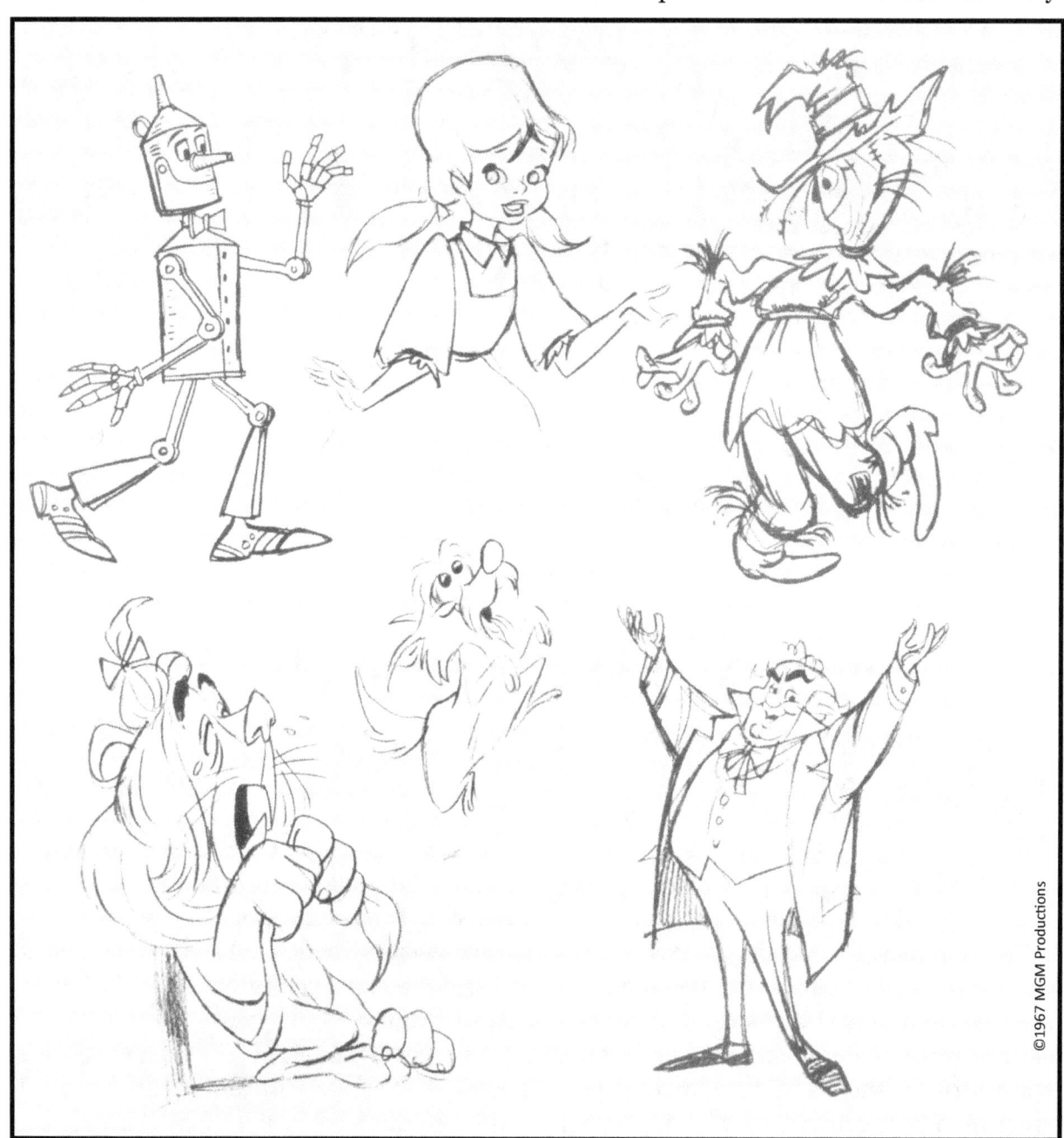

Original illustration for Chuck Jones' *Off To See The Wizard*, produced by MGM, 1967-68.

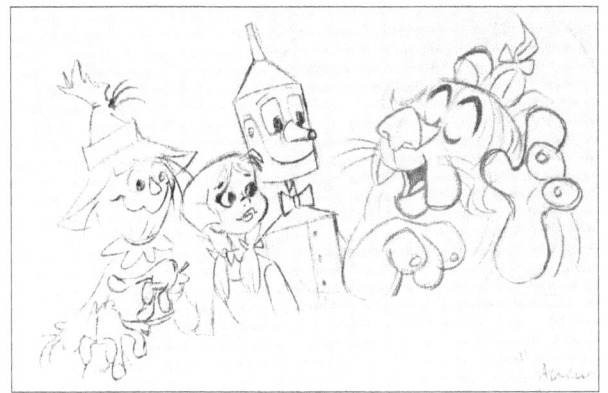 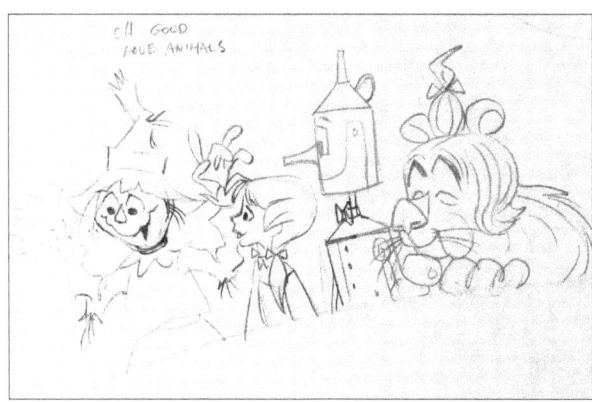

Pencil sketches for *Off To See The Wizard*, produced by MGM, 1967-68.

popular with young consumers of toys and games. A series of coloring books was published, puppets, and even a Scarecrow Jack-in-the-box.

Off To See The Wizard featured the top voice artists in the animation field. Mel Blanc performed the voice of the Cowardly Lion. June Foray did the voices for Dorothy and the Wicked Witch of the West. Daws Butler provided the voice of the Scarecrow and the Wizard. Don Messick performed the voices of the Tin Man and Toto.

Abe Levitow served as director of animation, with Earl Jonas as production manager. The animation staff included Hal Ambro, William Butler, Philip DeGuard, Don Foster, Ken Harris, Bob Inman, Volus Jones, Don Morgan, Maurice Noble, Bob Ogle, Phil Roman, Richard Thompson, Don Towsley, Ben Washam, and Thelma Witmer.

Films featured in the one-hour show were all MGM productions, such as *The Adventures of Huckleberry Finn, Flipper, Captain Sinbad* and *Who's Afraid of Mother Goose?* Due to the time restriction, the movies were divided in half, appearing as part one and part two in as many weeks.

Two episodes of *Off To See The Wizard* never made it to the airwaves, and lost with it were the tailored opening and closing Oz segments for the featured film. The film to be presented, *High Jungle*, was pulled from the line-up when actor Eric Fleming lost his life on September 28, 1966, due to drowning while filming a canoe scene on a turbulent river.

Off To See The Wizard is currently owned by Warner Brothers. It is unknown if any of the Oz segments will be released on DVD.

Some *Off To See The Wizard* opening and closing clips appear on YouTube, but are presented in black and white, not in their original Technicolor format.

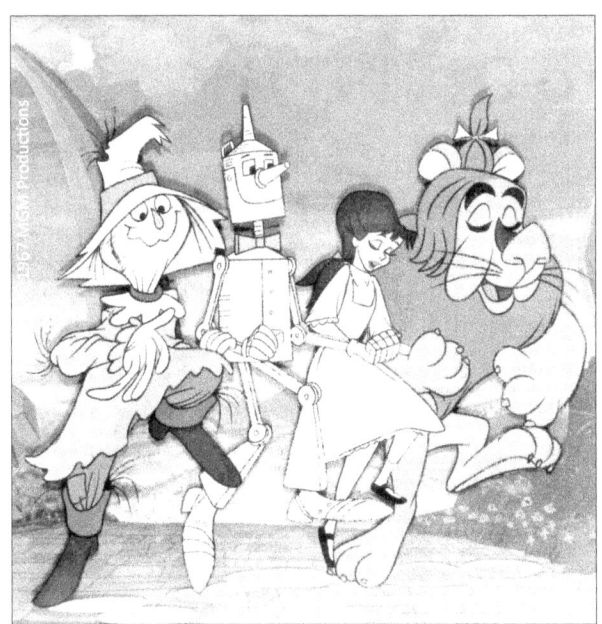

A scene from *Off To See The Wizard*.

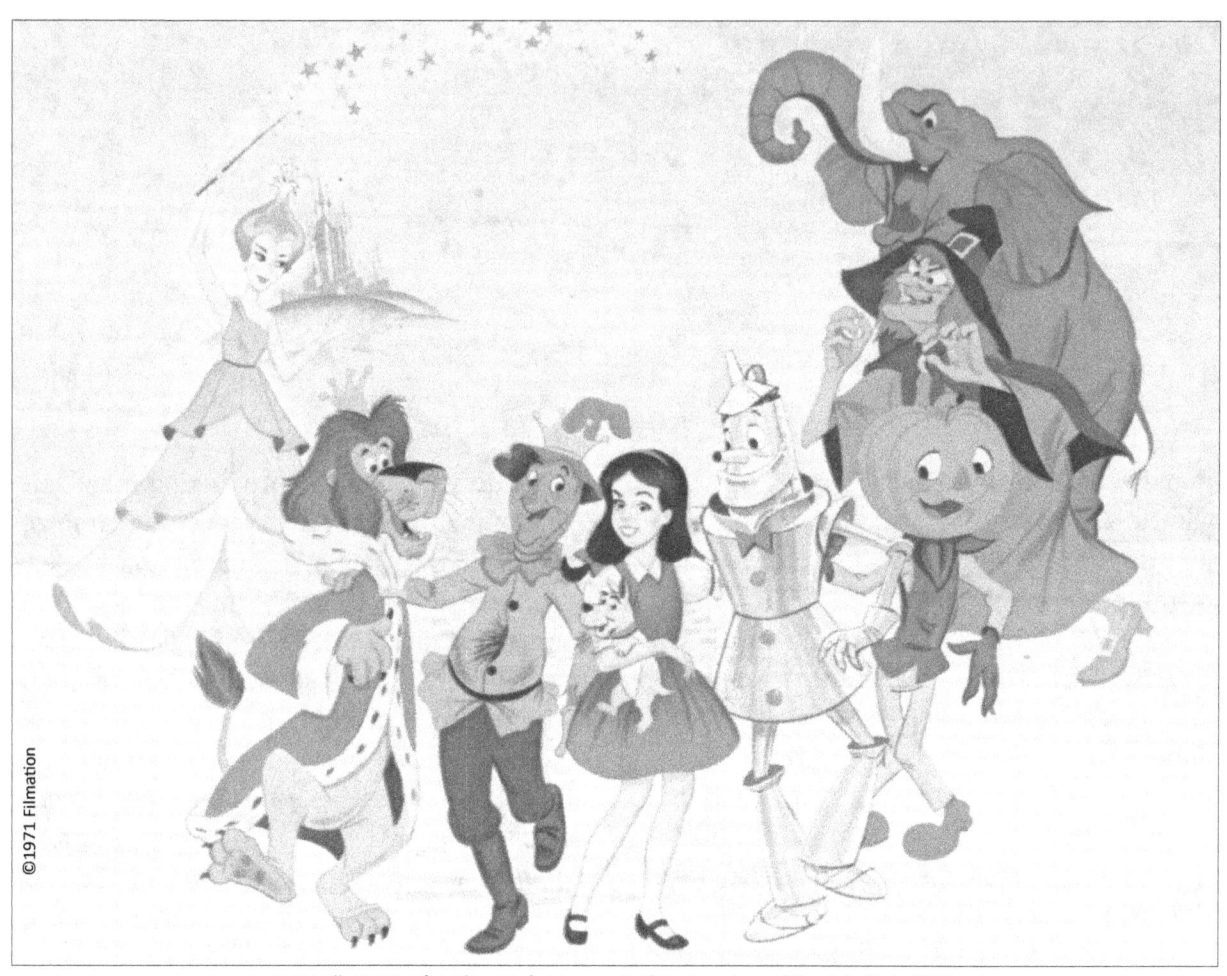

Poster illustration for Filmation's *Journey Back to Oz*, released theatrically in 1972.

Journey Back to Oz (1971)

Journey Back to Oz, a 1971 Filmation production, was the company's first feature-length animated film. The movie was released theatrically on December 14, 1972, in the United Kingdom. It made its theatrical debut in the United States in 1974, and subsequently appeared on the ABC television network in 1976, with comedian Bill Cosby, dressed as The Wizard, as the program host.

The project was initially intended to be a sequel to the 1939 MGM classic, *The Wizard of Oz*, which starred Judy Garland.

Interestingly, the character of the Wizard doesn't appear in *Journey Back to Oz*. Lyman Frank Baum's name is also absent from the film's credits. The story is scantly based on the author's *The Marvelous Land of Oz* book, but the Filmation feature doesn't mention Tip or Ozma, who both appeared in the book.

Initially announced as a co-production by Mike Santangelo and Lincoln Productions, the film entered pre-production in 1962, as Lou Scheimer and Hal Sutherland were forming the Filmation in Hollywood.

The voice recordings by an all-star cast were captured that year. But the project was

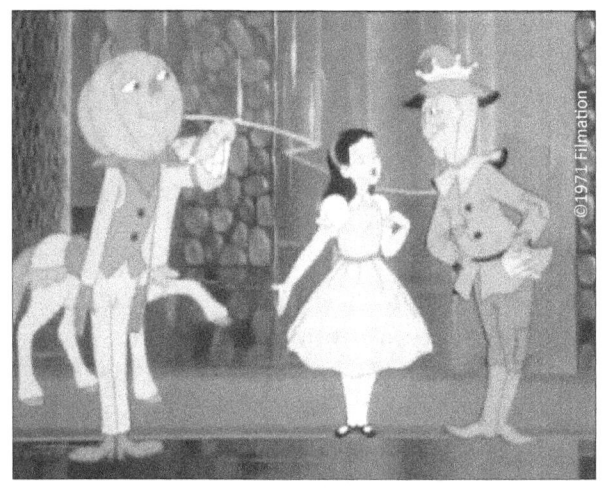

A scene from Filmation's *Journey Back to Oz*.

halted due to lack of financial resources after the completion of only a few minutes of animation. According to the September 2, 1963 issue of *Sponsor* magazine, its intended target release was to be April 1964.

Screenwriter Norm Prescott and co-writer Fred Ladd, who developed the script, made use of studios and resources connected to their production of Universal's *Pinocchio in Outer Space*.

"Norm had the idea that we could overlap some production with another picture, which turned out to be *Journey Back to Oz*," Ladd said in an interview. "The European studio was too small to accommodate this, so it was moved to Yugoslavia. They couldn't cut it and the picture was pulled from them. After a year, they still hadn't completed the six-minute prologue before the titles."

Curiosities concerning *Journey Back to Oz* include the voice of Dorothy being provided by Liza Minelli, the daughter of Judy Garland, and Margaret Hamilton, who played the Wicked Witch in the 1939 MGM classic, performing the voice of Aunt Em. Peter Lawford recorded the lines of the Scarecrow, but was replaced later by Mickey Rooney, after his voice was deemed too British.

Minelli's lines were recorded when she was age 15. Had the film been released during its initial production, it would have introduced the aspiring actress/singer in her first motion picture role.

It wasn't until profits rolled in from Filmation TV cartoon productions, such as *The Archies Show* and *The New Adventures of Superman*, that funds became available to reboot the Oz project.

The 1972 Filmation release, running 88-minutes, was directed by Hal Sutherland. It was written by Fred Ladd, Norm Prescott, and Bernard Evslin. The project was produced by Preston Blair, Fred Ladd, Lou Scheimer, and Prescott.

The soundtrack and songs were the invention of well-known composers Sammy Chan, Jimmy Van Heusen, and Walter Scharf.

Several big stars served as voice artists. Jack Pumpkinhead was played by comedian Paul Lynde. Herschel Bernardi played the Woodenhead Stallion. Ethel Merman was cast playing the voice of Mombi. Mickey Rooney was the Scarecrow, Danny Thomas the Tin Man, and Milton Berle played the Cowardly Lion.

Other voice artists included Rise Stevens as

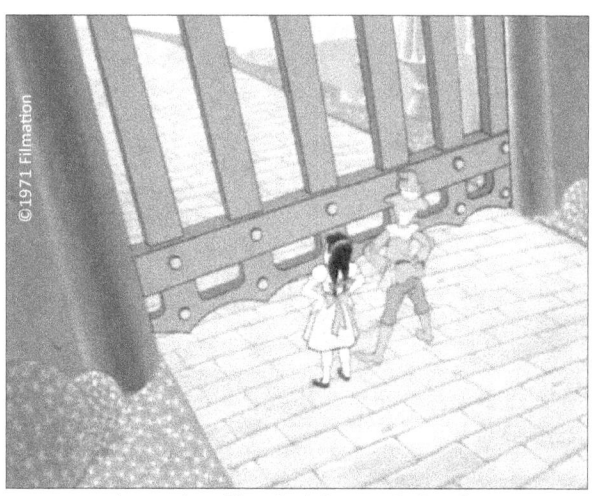

A scene from Filmation's *Journey Back to Oz*.

Glinda, Jack E. Leonard as the Signpost, Paul Ford as Uncle Henry, Don Messick as Toto, and Larry Storch, Dallas McKennon, and Mel Blanc in other roles.

Sherman Labby worked on the project as continuity storyboard artist. Animators, artists, and related personnel included Dale Baer, Don Bluth, Bob Bransford, Betty Brooks, Bob Carlson, Richie Craig, James Davis, Alberto De Mello, Otto Feuer, Dotti Foell, Ed Friedman, Fred Grable, Laverne Harding, C. L. Hartman, Maurice Harvey, Herb Hazelton, Mike Hazy, Lou Kachivas, Les Kaluza, Ervin Kaplan, Anatole Kirsanoff, George Kreisi, Paul Krukowski, Rudy Larriva, Phil Lewis, Bill Loudenslager, Bill Nunes, Jack Ozark, Amby Paliwoda, Manuel Perez, Don Peters, Jane Philippi, Virgil Raddatz, Rill Reed, John Remmel, Marjorie Roach, Virgil Ross, George Rowley, Ed Solomon, Ralph Somerville, Reuben Timmins, Don Towsley, Marion Tuck, Kay Wright, Paul Xander, Lou Zukor, and Phyllis Barnhart.

In the story, Dorothy and Toto are transported back to Oz after the girl is struck in the head by a fence gate. Dorothy and Toto encounter Mombi, the cousin of the deceased Wicked Witch of the West. She captures them. But they are soon freed by Jack Pumpkinhead.

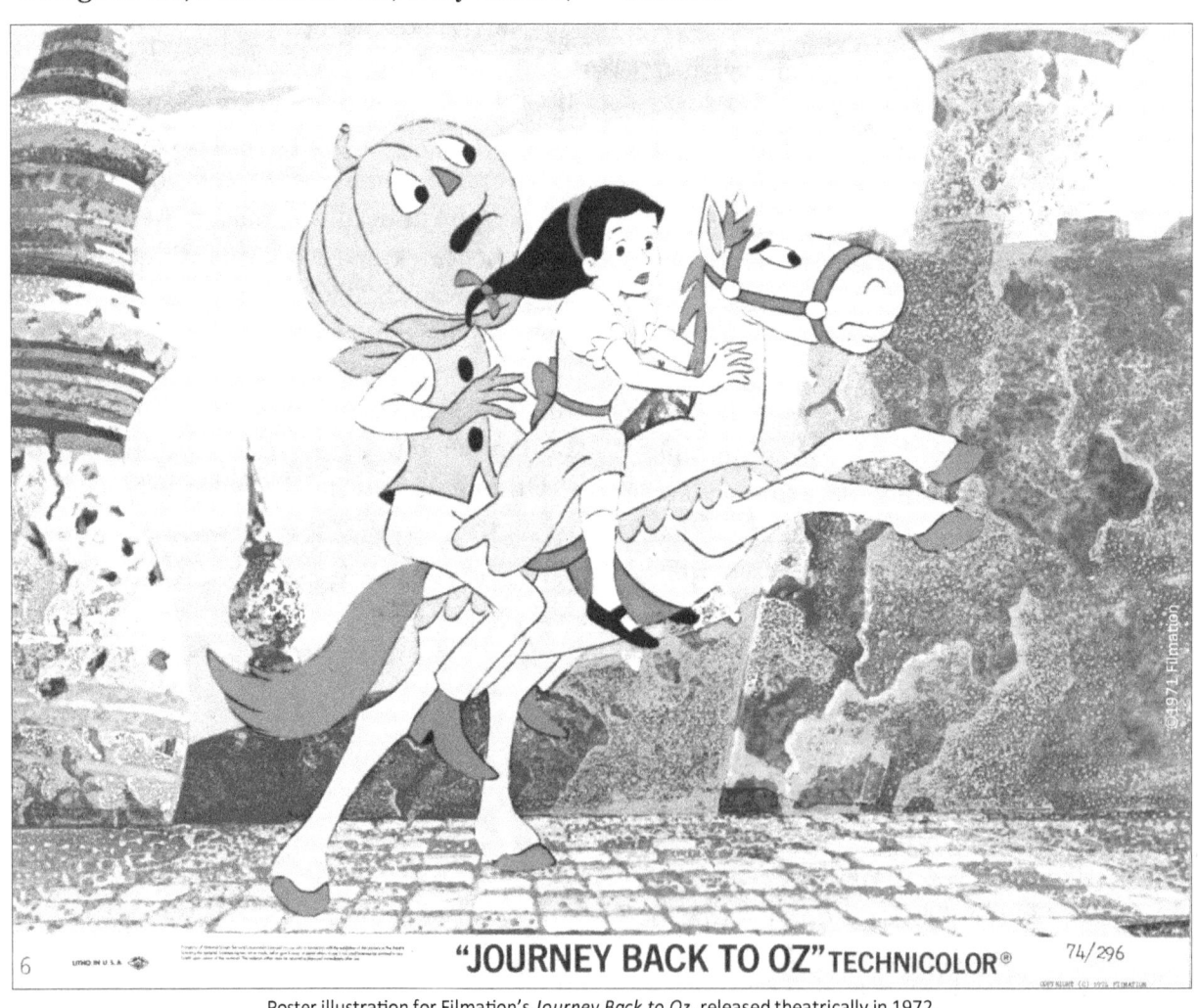

Poster illustration for Filmation's *Journey Back to Oz*, released theatrically in 1972.

We learn Mombi has created an army of Green Elephants, which she intends to use to overthrow the Emerald City and assume the throne.

Dorothy travels atop Woodhead Stallion, similar to the sawhorse depicted in Baum's book, *The Marvelous Land of Oz.* Arriving at The Emerald City, Jack and Dorothy inform the Scarecrow of Mombi's plot and the impeding elephant stampede.

Mombi arrives and captures Toto and the Scarecrow. Dorothy and Jack flee, seeking help from the Tin Man, who refuses due to his fear of the green pachyderms. They try to recruit the Lion next, but he backs out due to cowardice. Some friends they are!

Dorothy accepts a silver box from Glinda, the Good Witch, and instructs her not to opened it unless faced with an emergency.

The entire time, Mombi is watching the plans of the resistance by using a crystal ball. She uses a spell to give life to the forest trees, in an attempt to stop the rescue entourage. The effort fails, and the rescuers arrive at the city, where Dorothy opens the silver box, releasing mice that scare off the elephants.

Things rapidly spin out of control and Mombi is trampled by the stampeding elephants. The magic that made Jack Pumpkinhead come to life dies, too. But, he springs back to life by Dorothy's magical teardrops.

Dorothy and Toto are returned to Kansas via a tornado created by Glinda.

The film is stylish for a Filmation production, even with animation limitations.

The cast is colorful, distinctively depicted, and background illustrations are inventive and imaginative.

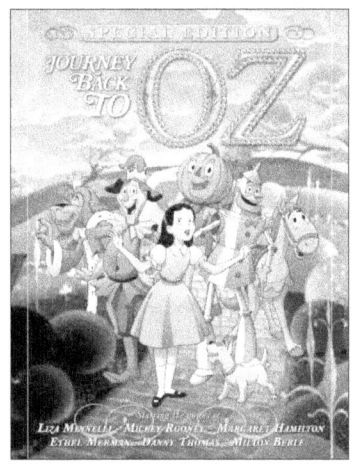
DVD of *Journey Back to Oz.*

However, *Journey Back to Oz* hardly represents the standards larger studios presented for animated theatrical films.

According to Norm Prescott, Filmation wanted to produce a "spin-off" of the feature as a network TV cartoon series, "but never got around to do it."

The theatrical version of the film was basically a flop. It only appeared in 11 theaters in the United States, according to one report.

Journey Back to Oz enjoyed popularity during its several rebroadcasts on television, last airing in 1984.

An original movie soundtrack album was released on vinyl, in 1980, by Texize. The record ran 38 minutes.

Bci/Eclipse released the full-length animated feature in DVD format on October 24, 2006.

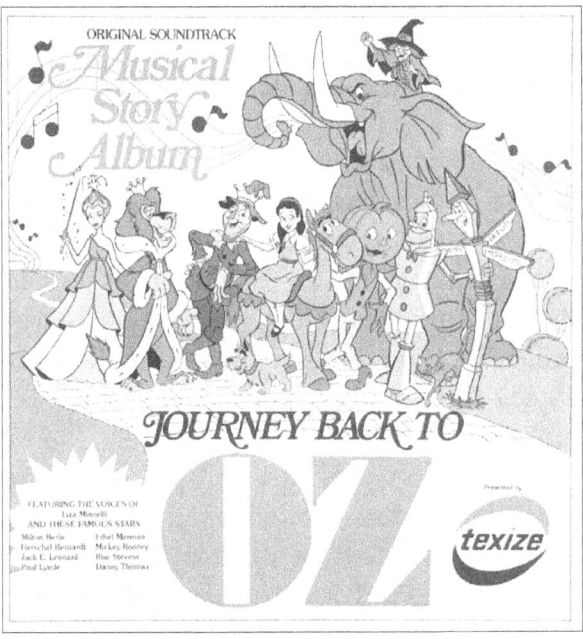
Soundtrack album of *Journey Back to Oz*, released in 1980.

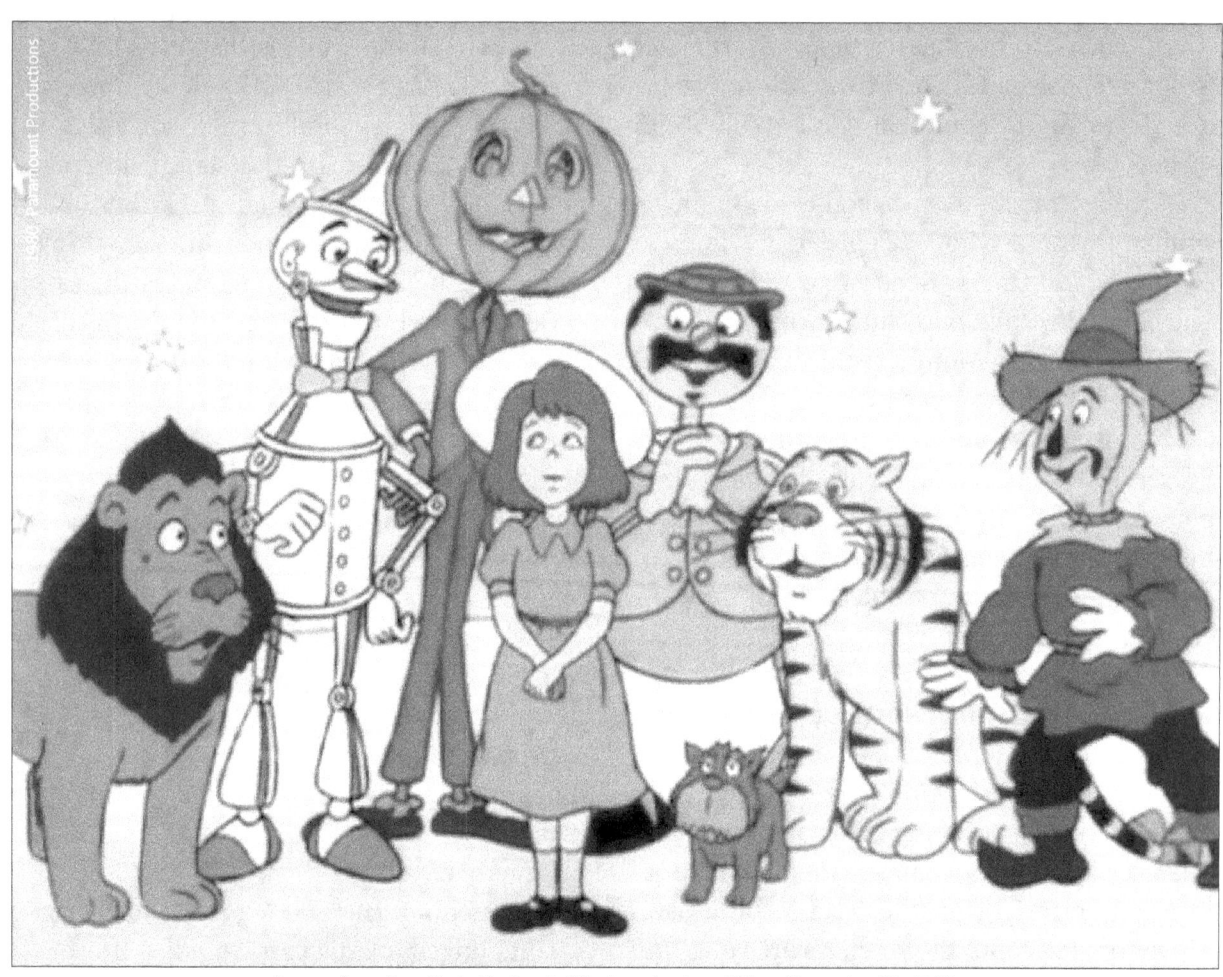

A scene from *Dorothy in the Land of Oz*, broadcast on CBS on November 25, 1980.

Dorothy in the Land of Oz (1980)

Dorothy in the Land of Oz is a made-for-television animated special produced by Murakami-Wolf-Swenson, Tôei Dôga Animation, and Muller-Rosen Productions. CBS first broadcast the program on November 25, 1980.

The cartoon, which runs 25 minutes, was initially titled *Thanksgiving in the Land of Oz*. The story was based on the Oz book *Dorothy and the Green Gobbler of Oz*, written by Romeo Muller, published by Scholastic in 1983. Characters showcased primarily were taken from Baum's *Ozma of Oz* and *The Emerald City of Oz* books.

Created as a Thanksgiving Day special, after its network premiere, the cartoon was re-edited leaving out any dialogue or visuals linking it to the holiday. It allowed for rebroadcast of the show at any time of the year. It next appeared in its re-edited form on CBS on December 10, 1981.

The cartoon presents Dorothy, Toto, the Wizard, U.N. Krust (Mince Pie), Jack Pumpkinhead, Tyrone the Terrible Toy Tinker, Nome King, Tik-Tok , Ozma, and the Hungry Tiger. Aunt Em and Uncle Henry are left be-

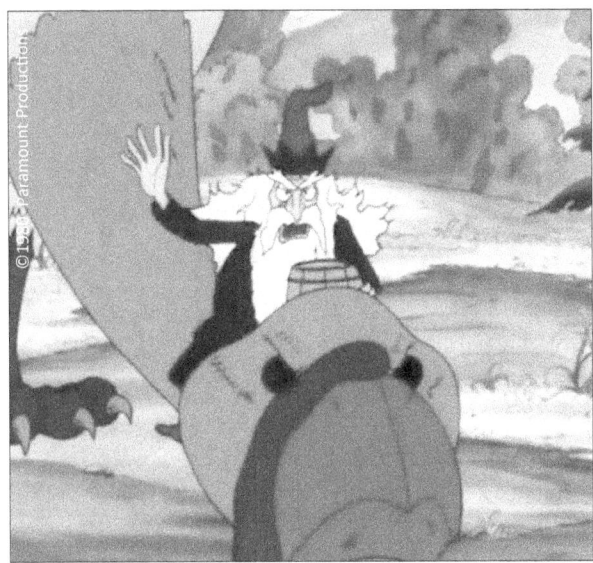

Tyrone the Terrible Toy Tinkerer.

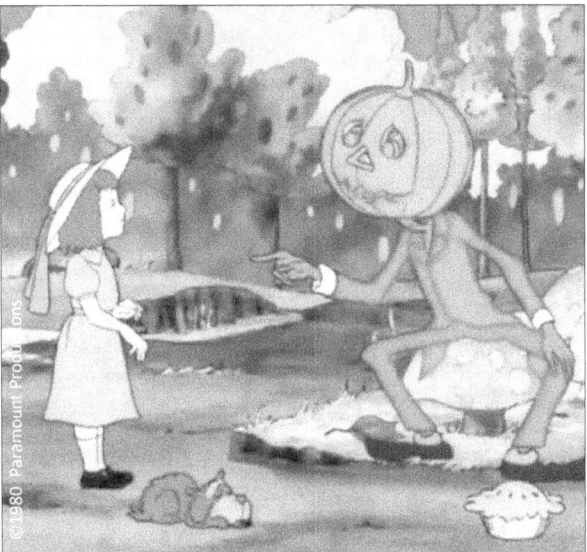

Dorothy meets Jack Pumpkinhead.

hind, of course, in Kansas.

In the cartoon, Dorothy is to spend Thanksgiving Day with her Aunt Em and Uncle Henry before their move to a retirement home. But it doesn't turn out that way initially when she is taken aloft in a green hot-air balloon, crafted in the design of a turkey, and transported to Oz.

Once there, she faces the threat of a character named Tyrone the Terrible Toy Tinkerer. The villain resembles The Gnome King in the style of second Baum Oz series artist, John R. Neill. The toy tinkerer has the ability to bring toys to life and command them for his evil purposes.

Tyrone brings the turkey balloon to life, creating a monster on the loose. Dorothy recruits Jack Pumpkinhead, The Hungry Tiger, and Tik-Tok to stop the evil madman.

The Scarecrow, Tin Man and Cowardly Lion make a cameo appearance at the conclusion of the story. Fans of Lyman Frank Baum's first book, *The Wonderful Wizard of Oz*, will notice that all three characters depicted are virtually identical and modeled after W. W. Denslow's illustrations.

Thus, stylistically, the cartoon pays tribute to W. W. Denslow and John R. Neill. Romeo Muller wrote *Dorothy in the Land of Oz*. Charles Swenson and Fred Wolf directed. Robert L. Rosen served as executive producer.

Producers included Romeo Muller, Charles Swenson, and Fred Wolf. The animation producer was Tomoo Fukumoto. Manager of the production was Kohsei Ohtani.

The artwork and character designs originated in Japan, Tomo Fukumoto served as

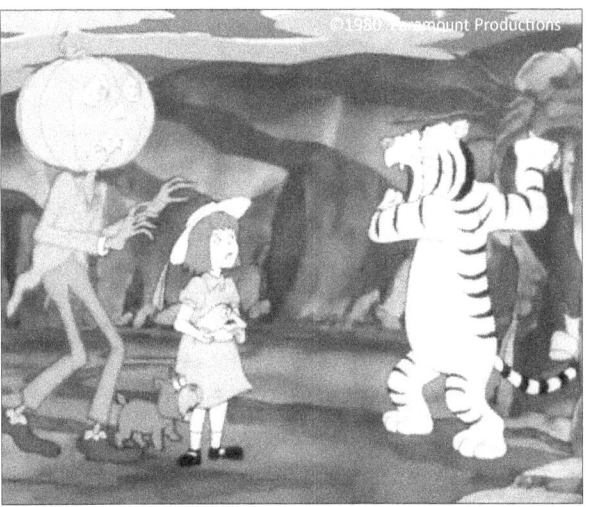

Dorothy and Jack Pumpkinhead meet Hungry Tiger.

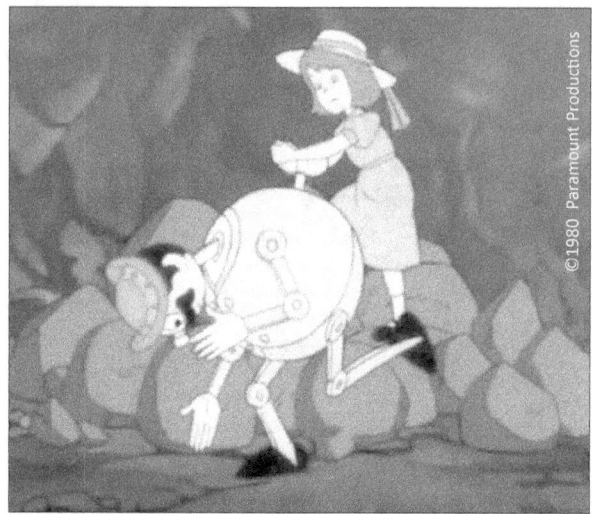

Dorothy winds up Tik-Tok, the mechanical man.

the animation producer with Takashi Abe as director of the animation. Kohsei Ohtani was production manager. The film editor was Chikako Matsubara.

Animators and illustrators included Tosho Mori, Tatsui Kino, Toyohiko Hiraga, Paro Hozumi, Tsutomu Tsukada and Tsutomu Tsukada.

Romeo Muller wrote the story and lyrics for songs. Stephen Lawrence provided the music, with additional scores supplied by David Campbell.

Many actors and voice artists made up the

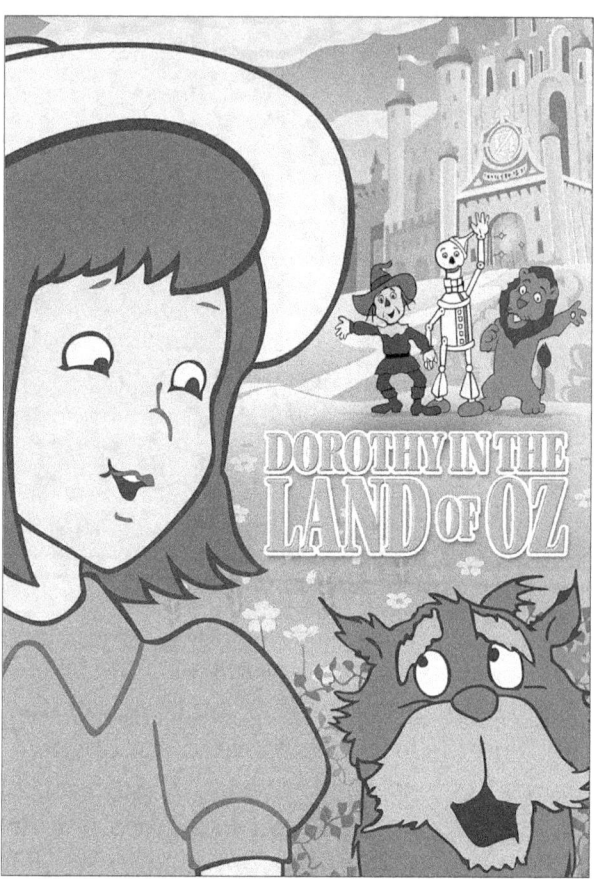

Cover of Paramount's 2015 DVD release.

colorful cast. Emmy-award winning TV comedian Sid Caesar narrated the story, playing the Wizard, and U.N. Krust. Mischa Bond played Dorothy, Robert Ridgely provided voices for Jack Pumpkinhead, Tyrone the Terrible Toy Tinker, and the Nome King. Joan Gerber provided the voice for Tik-Toc, and Ozma, with Frank Nelson as the Hungry Tiger, Lurene Tuttle as Aunt Em, and Charles Woolf as Uncle Henry, Maitzi Morgan, and Julie Cohen.

MGM Video released the cartoon on Betamax tape in the early 1980's. Best Film and Video Company released the program on VHS tape in 1993.

Liberation Entertainment first issued the program on DVD in 2007, with Paramount reissuing the cartoon on DVD in 2015.

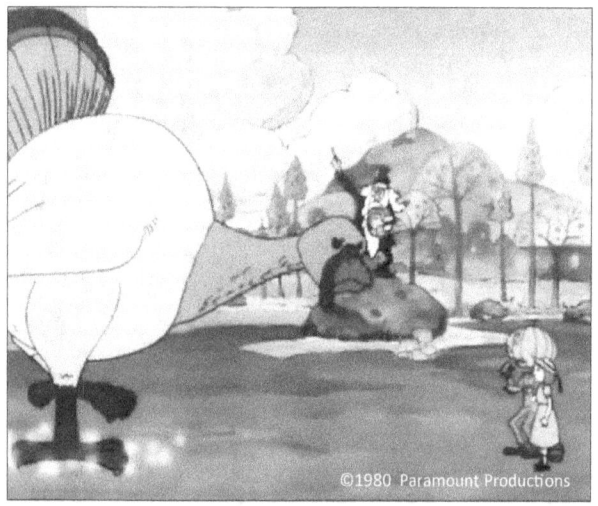

The green turkey balloon comes to life.

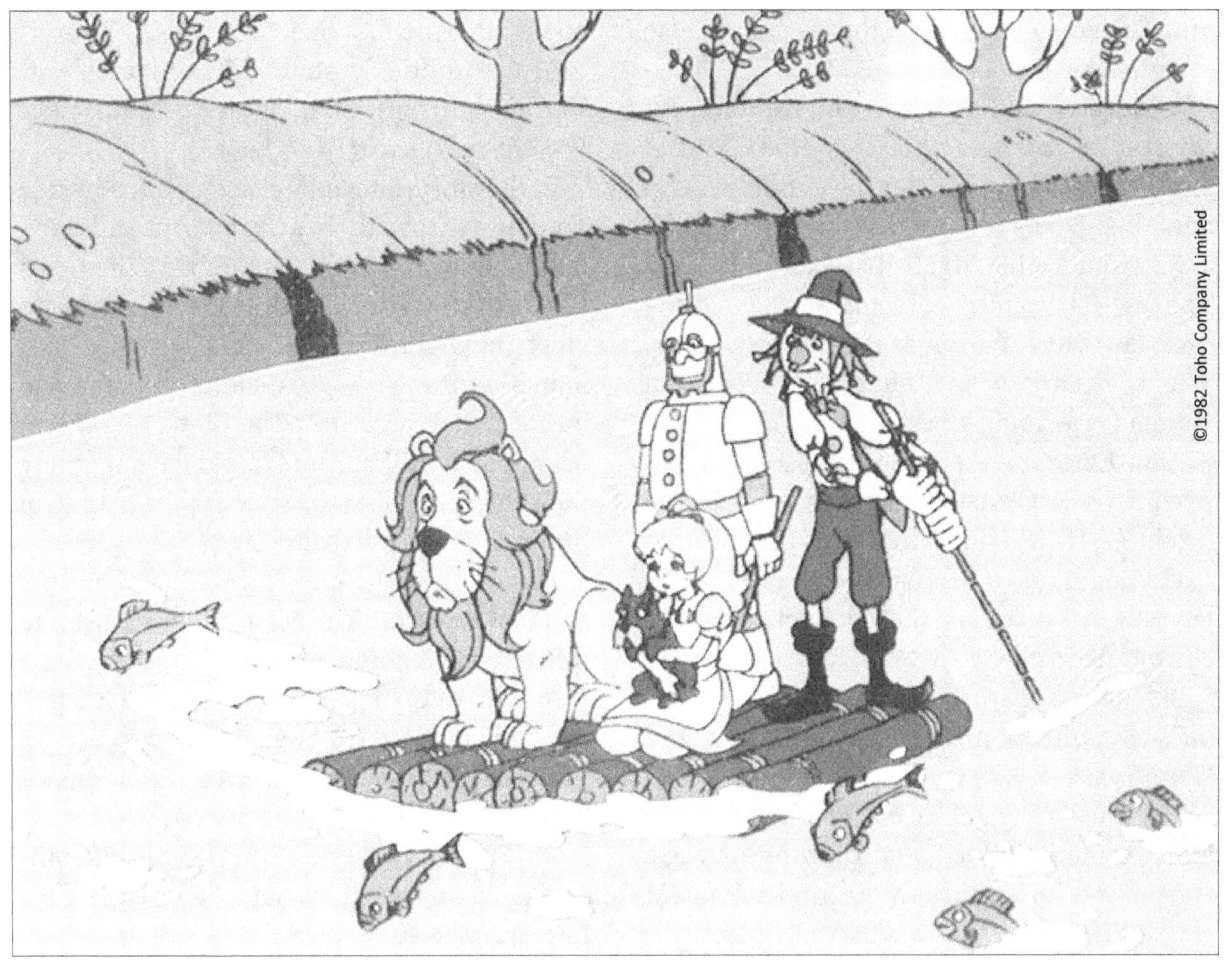

A scene from Toho's *The Wizard of Oz* feature-length cartoon, released in North America in 1982.

The Wizard of Oz (1982)

The Wizard of Oz is a 1982 adaptation of Lyman Frank Baum's first Oz book, produced by Yoshimitsu Banno and Katsumi Ueno for Toho Company Limited (Japan), released on May 31, 1982. The cartoon first appeared on North American television on October 6, 1982 in North America, then briefly appeared in select U.S. theaters.

The 78-minute feature-length cartoon, that was shown at the Cannes Film Festival, did not enjoy much theatrical success in America, and wasn't released in Japan until 1986.

The film, directed by Fumihiko Takayama, presented a screenplay by Banno and Akira Miyazaki.

The Wizard of Oz was initially recorded in English, and it wasn't until later, when it was released in Japan in 1986, that dialogue was in Japanese. Voice artists in that version included talents such as Mari Okamoto, Kotobuki Hizuru, Jōji Yanami, and Masashi Amenomori.

It subsequently was also dubbed in the Slovak language, as well as Italian and Greek.

The initial English speaking cast included veteran actor Lorne Greene as the Wizard, and Aileen Quinn as Dorothy. Quinn also sang the songs in the feature.

It featured the original compositions, *It's Strictly Up to You, I Dream of Home*, and *A Wizard of a Day*, written by Sammy Cahn and Allen Byrns.

Providing other English voices were Billy Van as the Scarecrow, John Stocker as the Tin Man, Thick Wilson as the Cowardly Lion, Wendy Thatcher as Glinda, and Elizabeth Hanna performing several character voices.

Alan Enterprises produced the English aspect, Alan L. Gleitsman serving as executive producer, with John Danylkiw as producer.

Key animator on the project was Koji Kobayashi. Art direction was conducted by Shichiro Kobayashi.

Shichiro Kobayashi subsequently worked on such animation series as *The Littles* and *The Mighty Orbots*.

The movie stays close to the original Baum story. Glinda is added, and Dorothy's "magic shoes," red in color, borrows from the MGM classic. The cartoon also artistically pays tribute to some of the style seen in John R. Neill's drawings, who illustrated a slew of Oz books after the first one.

Critics routinely state this animated version is the truest adaptation of Baum's *The Wonderful Wizard of Oz* book.

In the story, a tornado sweeps Dorothy and Toto away from their Kansas farmland, having them awake in the land of Oz. The Good Witch of the North sends her on her way to meet the Wizard to help find her way back home. As the story goes, along the road she meets the Scarecrow, Tin Man, and Lion, who join her. Each are seeking something they think is missing, which is not, that of brains, a heart, and courage.

There's the attack by the Kalidah, and the scene where the Tin Man chops down the tree to cross a gorge.

At Emerald City, each in the party, separately, is granted an audience with the Wizard. They all see different manifestations of him.

Only Dorothy sees a giant head, while others see a beautiful woman, a beast, and a flaming sphere.

Tasked with destroying the Wicked Witch of the West to achieve their personal desires,

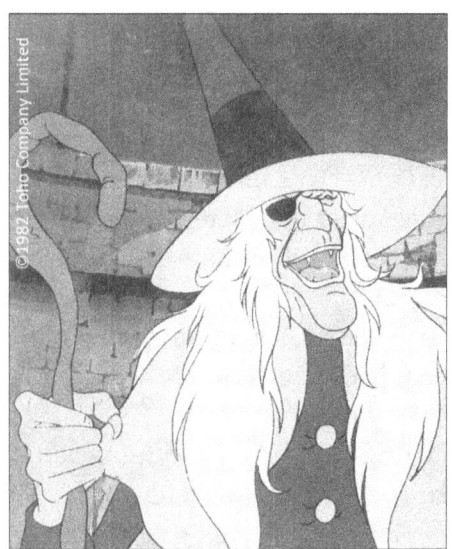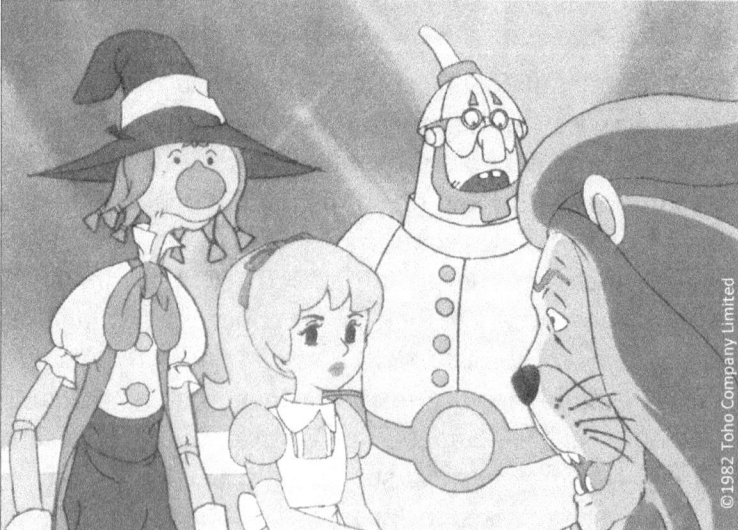

The Wicked Witch, and Dorothy and her friends, in scenes from Toho's *The Wizard of Oz* feature-length cartoon.

the team sets off on their way to her castle. The evil witch has gray skin and hair, and wears an eyepatch.

They confront a pack of magical wolves, some crows, and render the enemies' defeat. However, a swarm of winged monkeys capture Dorothy and her troupe.

Once a captive in the castle, Dorothy refuses to give the witch her magical shoes.

In the end, Dorothy topples a large jug of water down steps and into the path of the witch. She melts and her evil soldiers vanish. Her slaves, the Winkies, are freed.

Back at Emerald City, reporting to the Wizard, the true identity of the ruler is revealed to be a washed-up former circus magician.

He explains what the Scarecrow, Tin Man and Lion that what they sought they pos-

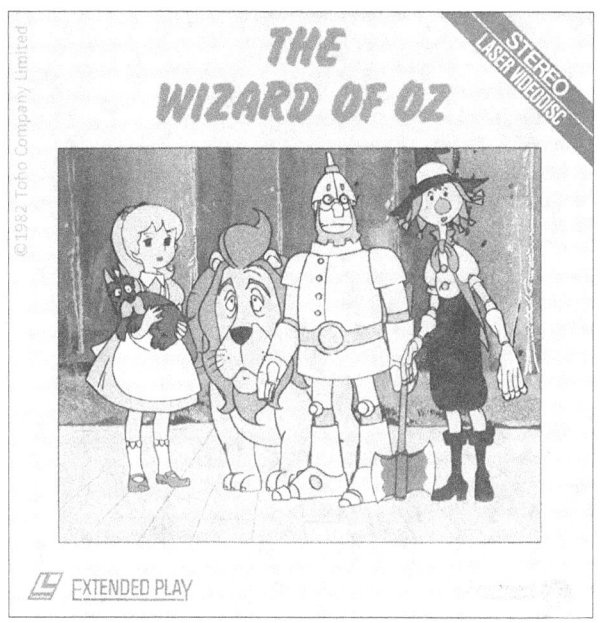

The Laserdisc release of the film in the 1980's.

sessed all along. Then he fails to return Dorothy to Kansas when his hot air balloon carries him aloft alone.

Glinda appears and reminds Dorothy her shoes possess the power to return her and Toto, and with a click of her heels, they return home.

Toho's *The Wizard of Oz* is one of the finest cartoon depictions of Baum's Oz, taking scant creative liberties, such as Dorothy with blonde hair, but remains loyal to the author's vision. The artwork is simple, yet presents appealing characterizations. The backgrounds are attractive, and the animation is indicative of finer made-for-TV cartoons, but smooth in execution.

Paramount Home Video released the movie in English on VHS, Betamax, Laserdisc and CED in the 1980's for the home video market. The film appears on DVD as *Ozu no mahôtsukai*, not in English, but Polish and Japanese, and not playable on U.S. devices. The feature does appear on YouTube.

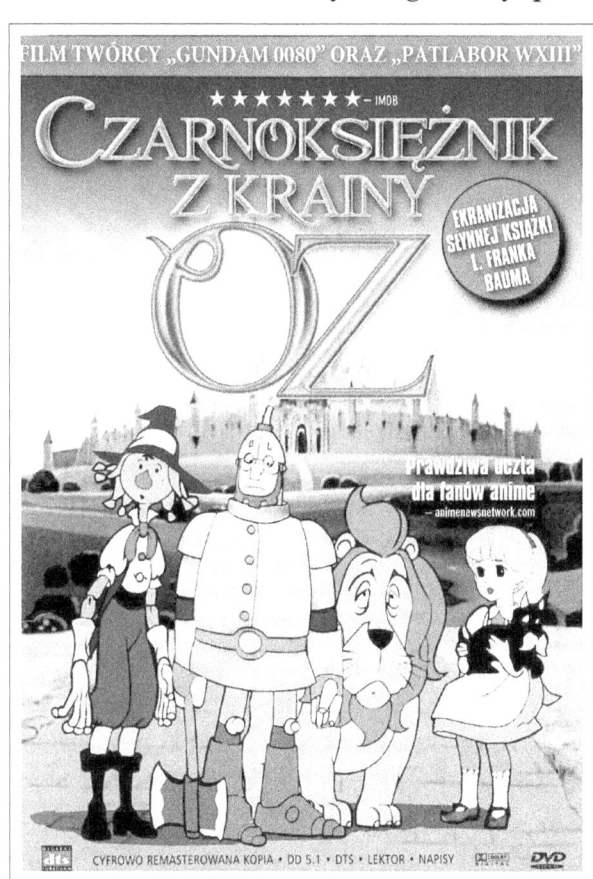

The only DVD currently available of the film.

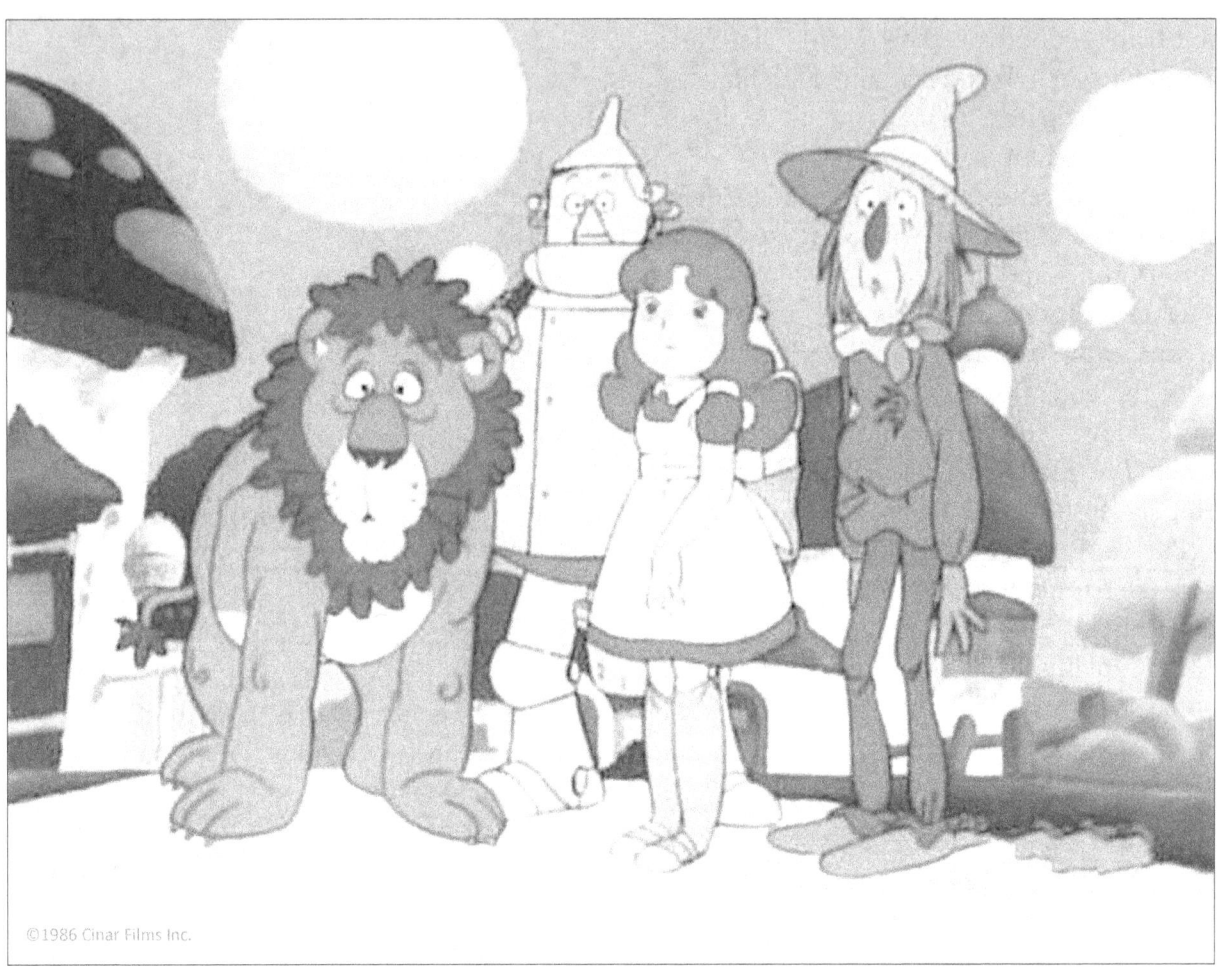

Cinar Films' *The Wonderful Wizard of Oz* series spanned 52 episodes, and was edited into four movies.

The Wonderful Wizard of Oz (1986)

The Wonderful Wizard of Oz was the first installment of four feature-length animated movies released in 1987, by Cinar Films Inc. The content from all four Cinar Oz features came from a Japanese anime series titled *Oz no Mahōtsukai (Wizard of Oz)*, produced by Enoki Films Company. Ltd. Enoki turned out 52 episodes from 1986-87.

The original series was produced by Tetsuro Kumase, and directed by Hiroshi Saito and Masaru Tonogouchi. The characters were designed by Shuichi Seki, with Yoichi Kotabe serving as director of animation.

The television series told four different Oz tales. The first, spanning episodes 1-17, presented *The Wonderful World of Oz*. It was followed by *The Marvelous Land of Oz* (episodes 18-30), *Ozma of Oz* (episodes 31-41), and *The Emerald City of Oz* (episodes 42-52).

In 1987, HBO purchased the rights to the series and contracted with Cinar Films Inc. of Montreal, Canada, to produce English versions of the series, editing them into four feature-length movies. Cinar, founded in 1976, was heavily involved in the production of programs for children.

Cinar's western version of *The Wonderful Wizard of Oz* was released in 1987. Subsequent movies in the series included *The Marvelous Land of Oz*, *Ozma of Oz*, and *The Emerald City of Oz*, all based on the original titles by Lyman Frank Baum.

The English version wipes out the names of any Japanese talents involved in the original series, including several dozen voice actors.

The story, rewritten by Don Ariolo and Tim Reid, pretty much remains true to the original Baum book series.

Cinar's *The Wonderful Wizard of Oz* series was produced by Ronald A. Weinberg, with he and Micheline Charest serving as executive producers. Elizabeth Klinck was an associate producer. The technical producer was Jacques Pettigrew. Production advisors included Dov Zimmer and Claude Fournier. The film was directed by Tim Reid.

The post production supervisor was Pierre Michaud, assisted by coordinator Liz Joyce.

Gerald Potterton was the director of animation, with Christine Larocque as animation supervisor. Elaine Gasco was in charge of storyboards. Ian MacGillivray was the animation camera supervisor.

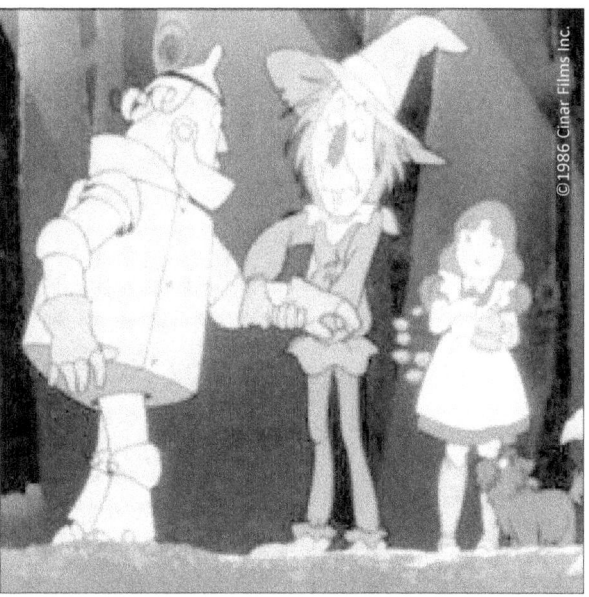

A scene from Cinar's Oz series.

Animators on the movie include Nik Ranieri, Maldwyn Phillips, Nancy Crossgrove, Raymond Furlotte, Pierre Houde, Elaine Gasco and Cine-Titre. Alex Simard was the director of color. Avde Chiraeff as the supervising picture editor, with Laurent LeClerc assisting.

The supervising sound editor was Raymond Vermette, assisted by Tony Reed, Ian Rankin, Daniel Vincent and Gilles Page. Music editors included Richard Homme, Tom Szczesniak and Ray Parker. The sound engineers were Gaetan DePelteau and Ron Searles. Rerecording was supervised by Sheely Craig and Andre Gilles Gagne.

Monique Bergeron was the talent coordinator. Narration for the cartoon was performed by actress Margot Kidder, best known for her role as Lois Lane in the Christopher Reeve *Superman* movies.

Providing the voices of primary characters was Morgan Hallet as Dorothy, George Morris as the Tin Man, Neil Shee as the Lion, and

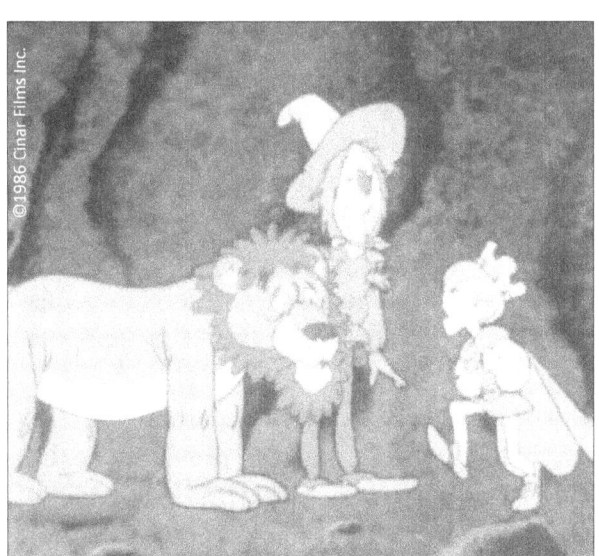

A scene from Cinar's Oz series.

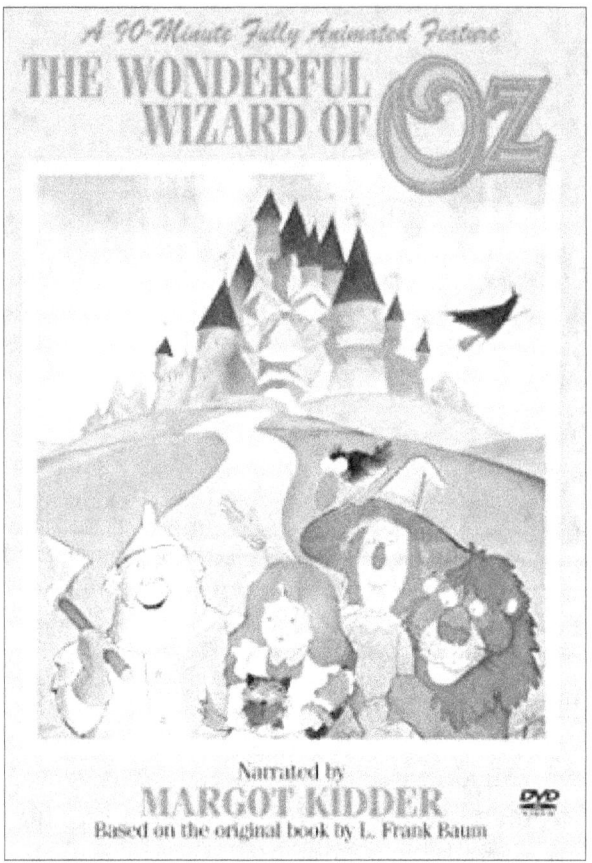

The first Cinar *Oz* series edit released as a feature-length movie.

Richard Dumont as the Scarecrow.

Other voices appearing include Steven Bednarski, Harvey Berger, Maria Bircuer, Mark Denis, Kathleen Fee, Carol Ann Francis, Gayle Garfinkle, Susan Glover, Arthur Grosser, Dean Hagopian, A. J. Henderson, Adrian Knight, Terrence LaBrosse, Linda Lonn, Liz MacRae, Bronwen Mantel, Walter Massey, Gordor Masten, Steve Michaels, Carla Napier, Linda O'Dwyer, Barbara Pogemiller, Rob Roy, Michael Rudder, Howard Ryshpan, Vlasta Vrana, Tim Webber, and Jane Woods.

The music was composed by Hagood Hardy, Tom Szczesnaik, and Ray Parker, and performed by Szczesniak, Hardy, Parker, Richard Homme, Brian Leonard, Robert Piltch, and Jack Zaza. The song "Searching for a Dream" was performed by The Parachute Club.

Perhaps the worst thing about Cinar's *The Wonderful Wizard of Oz* series is the drab, uninspired narration by Margot Kidder. However, some critics give Kidder high marks for her narration work.

The first stretch of the series, *The Wonderful World of Oz* (episodes 1-17), tells the traditional tale based on the first Baum Oz book.

The Marvelous Land of Oz (episodes 18-30) introduces Princess Ozma, who, under enchantment, has been transformed into a boy named Tip. Ozma discovers her true identity after adventures involving the Scarecrow, Jack Pumpkinhead, the Sawhorse, the Scarecrow, and others in Oz. This adventure also included the song, "Listen to your Heart," performed by The Parachute Club.

In *Ozma of Oz* (episodes 31-41), Dorothy returns to the Land of Oz and runs into the nasty Wheelers, and a mechanical man named Tik Tok. Dorothy is reunited with the Scarecrow, Tin Woodsman, and the Lion, and meets Ozma, the Princess of Oz, who all join her on a mission to help save the Royal Family of Ev.

In *The Emerald City of Oz* (episodes 42-52), the Nome King seeks revenge against the citizens of Oz, who defeated him in the previous adventure. With assistance from Guph, a trained invader, the Nome King and his army tunnel beneath the Deadly Desert on a mission to make slaves of Emerald City's population.

The entire Cinar series is perhaps the best animated representations of Baum's first three, and sixth Oz books. One critic said of the entire series that it may not be the best animated Oz work, but is most loyal to the

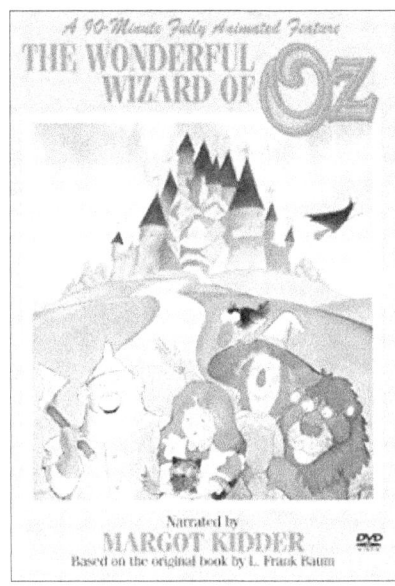 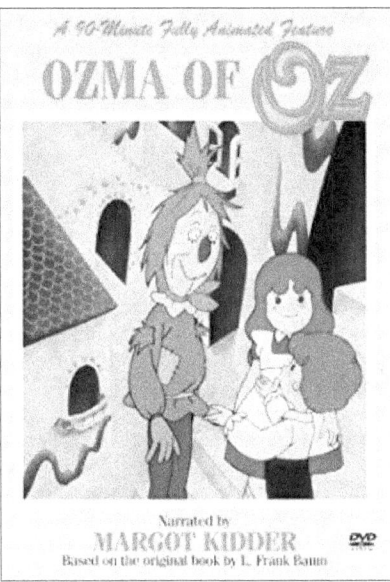 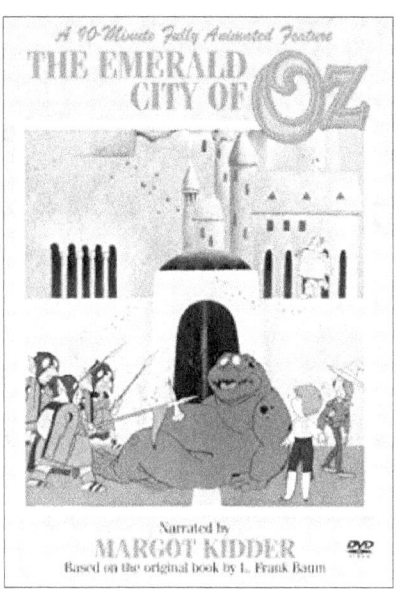

The three other Cinar *Oz* series edits released as feature-length movies.

original books.

In 2004, Lightyear Video released all four movies individually, and in a boxed set, featuring all four. In 2017, Sony Entertainment released a 2-DVD 25th Anniversary Collection that included al four movies.

On August 29, 2017, Discotek Media released all 52 episodes in the series on Blu-ray. However, this collection has been criticized because it is all compacted onto one disc. The overall average picture quality of the cartoon isn't what many Blu-ray customers expected.

Cinar's The Wizard of Oz Episode Guide

Dorothy Meets the Munchkins / Dorothy Finds a Friend / Adventures Along the Yellow Brick Road / The Journey to the Emerald City / Saved by the Mouse Queen / The Emerald City at Last / The Wizard Wants a Favor / The Wicked Witch of the West / Dorothy's Magic Powers / Freedom from the Witch / Mombi, Tip and the Golden Cap / Back to the Emerald City / The Wizard's Disappointing Secret / The Wizard Tries to Help / Journey to the South / Glinda, the Good Witch / Home Sweet Home Again / Dorothy Meets the Wizard Again / Back to Oz / Escape from Mombi / General Jinjur Attacks / Escape from the Emerald City / Tin Man to the Rescue / Mombi's Terrible Magic / Trapped in the Palace / The Magical Escape / Glinda Agrees to Help / The Emerald City Captured / Mombi's Attempt to Trick Glinda / Ozma, Princess of Oz / Tick Tok the Mechanical Man / The Kidnapped Prince / The Deadly Desert / The Talking Hen / Monsters of Stone / The Underground Country of Nomes / The Deadly Guessing Game / Dorothy Outsmarts the King / The Secret Fear of the Nomes / The Nome King Sets a Trap / Saved by the Sun / The Nome King Plans Revenge / Princess Ozma's Secret / Miss Cuttenclip and Mister Fuddle / The Growleywog Joins the Nomes / Water of Oblivion / Nomes on the March / A Winky Helps His King / The Crowning of Ozma / The Nomes Attack / Dorothy and Her Friends Defend the Palace / A Very Happy Ending.

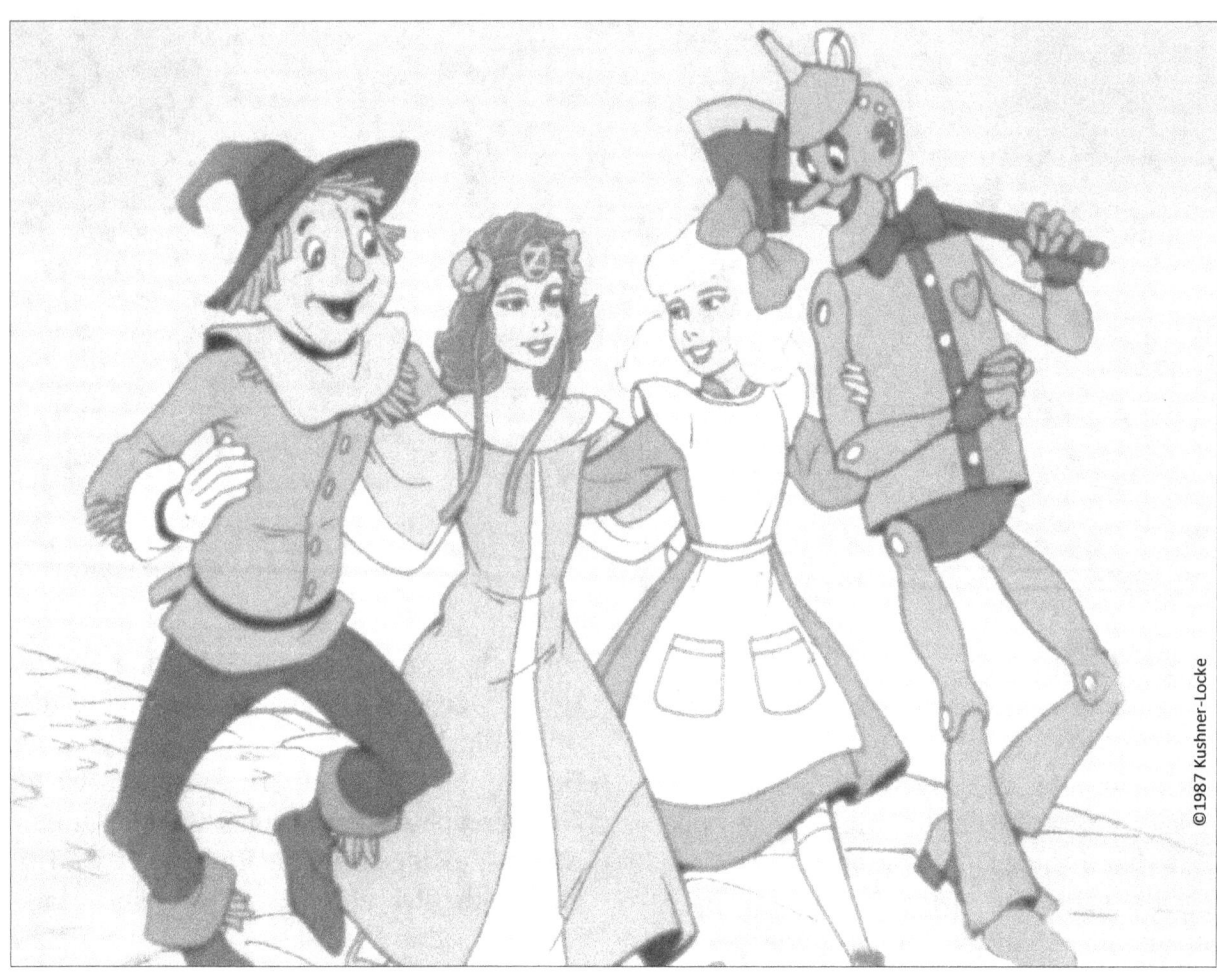

Promotional illustration for Kushner-Locke's *Dorothy Meets Ozma of Oz*, 1987.

Dorothy Meets Ozma of Oz (1987)

Dorothy Meets Ozma of Oz is a 1987 adaptation of Lyman Frank Baum's book *Ozma of Oz*, produced by The Kushner-Locke Company for Lorimar Television. The 28-minute cartoon was released directly into the home video market.

Actor Michael Gross, star of the TV show *Family Ties*, introduces and closes the cartoon, in live-action segments.

While speculation, it's likely Gross cringes at his participation in the project. His enthusiastic introduction merely sets the viewer up for the biggest animated disappointment in Oz cartoon history. Not only is the story beyond lame, the character art and modeling is unattractive and out of proportion, but strikingly nondescript and downright ugly.

Voice actors onboard were Sandra Butcher, Nancy Chance, Jay David, Janice Kawaye, Fredie Smootie and Matthew Stone.

Janice Kawaye, who did the voice of Dorothy, is the only voice artist that subsequently appeared in other TV and motion picture productions. Kawaye's voice appeared in the animated series *Beavis and Butthead*, *Captain Planet and the Planeteers*, *Invader Zim*,

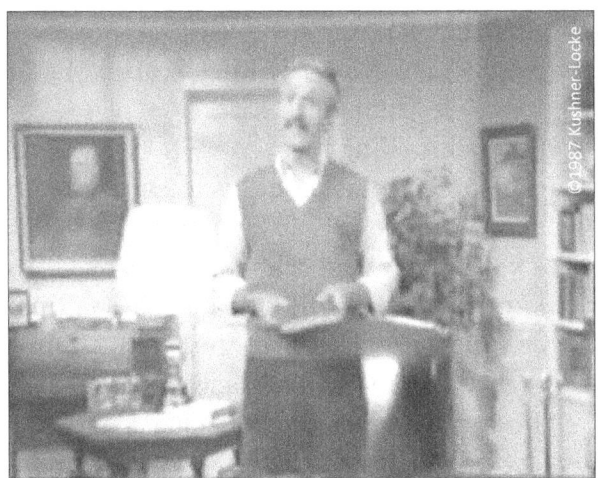 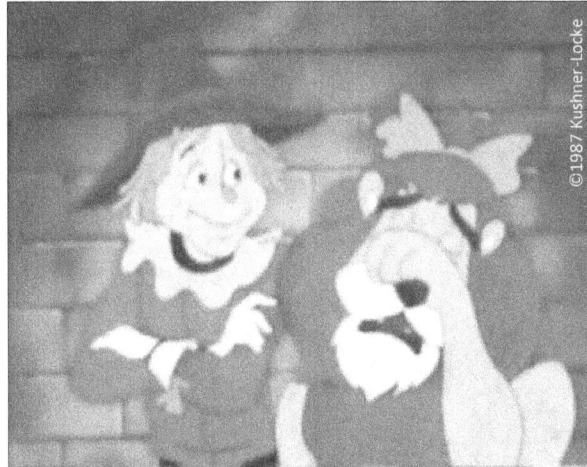

Michael Gross, left, and the Scarecrow and Cowardly Lion, in scenes from Kushner-Locke's *Dorothy Meets Ozma of Oz*, 1987.

and *My Life as a Teenage Robot*.

It's not surprising the other voice artists appear to have vanished from the entertainment business. *Dorothy Meets Ozma of Oz* would even make a toddler vomit.

The executive producers of the cartoon were Donald Kushner and Peter Locke, with assistant producers Thomas Bliss, Diana Dru Botsford, and Traci Graham-Rice. Management producers were Ellyn Friedman and Nelson Shin.

The story was written by Jim Carlson and Terrence McDonnel. The animation and art department was comprised of Richie Chavez, Kit Harper, Jim Mitchell, Andrew Phillipson, Mike Stribling, Donald Towns, Timothy Burgard, Greg Davidson and Phillip Norwood.

Directors of animation included Myrna Bushman, Joe Cisi, Pierre DeCelles, George Grammat, Bill Knoll, Chiou Wen Shian and Lisa Wilson. Art director on the project was Phillip Felix. Directing actor Michael Gross' live action scenes was Thomas A. Bliss, assisted by James Carhart.

Casting was conducted by Brenda Kyle, with music by Joel Hirschhorn, Al Kasha, and Michael Lloyd.

In the story, Dorothy and Toto are swept overboard while on a voyage to Australia with Aunt Em and Uncle Henry. Nothing like getting away from the old farmhouse in Kansas and running up the credit cards for a voyage. Ma and Pa Kettle go on vacation!

Dorothy, who is a blonde in this production, not a brunette, and her dog Toto, are swept overboard. Sadly, they survive. Dorothy washes ashore in a crate with a talking chicken named Billina. Then she encounters the Wheelers, basically jerks with wheels where their hands and feet should be.

The Wheelers are obnoxious, and chase Dorothy, Billina, and Toto around. Coming

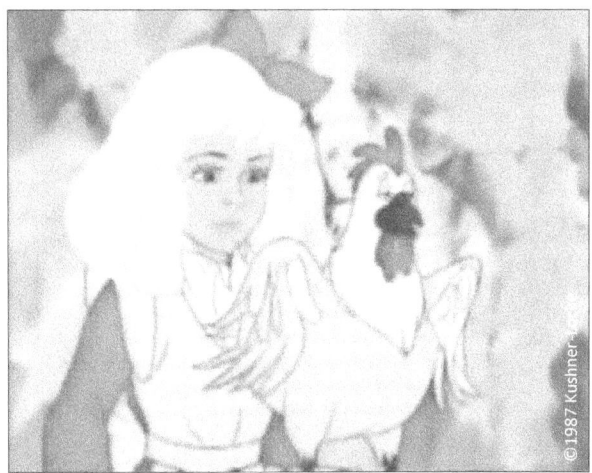

Dorothy and Billina, in *Dorothy Meets Ozma of Oz*.

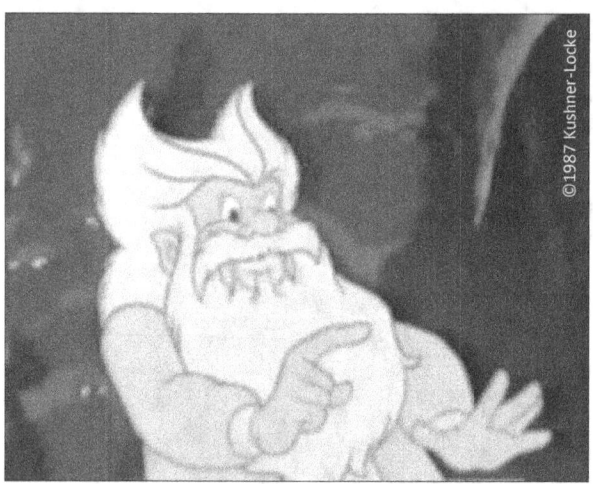

The Nome King, in *Dorothy Meets Ozma of Oz*.

to break up the calamity are the Tin Man, Scarecrow, Cowardly Lion, the Hungry Tiger, Princess Ozma, and Tik-Tok, the mechanical man.

The entourage embarks on a mission to the Land of The Nome King. The evil ruler has kidnapped Queen Ev and her ten kids. Dorothy and her friends are determined to free her and her children. The King wears a Magical Belt giving him powers.

The Nome King has been transforming people into ornaments for his treasure room. The Tin Man, Lion, Tiger, Scarecrow, and Tik-Tok soon join his collection.

Dorothy, Ozma, and Billina arrive, putting an end the evil schemes of the tyrant. Dorothy strips the King of his magical belt, restoring his captives, including the Queen and her children, to their original state. She also uses the belt to return to Kansas.

The cartoon is hard to watch because it is so idiotic and substandard, even compared to some of the worst animated cartoons of the 1980's. It is more than likely the worst cartoon based on *The Wizard of Oz* ever made.

Lorimar released the cartoon in VHS format in 1987. It has never appeared on DVD.

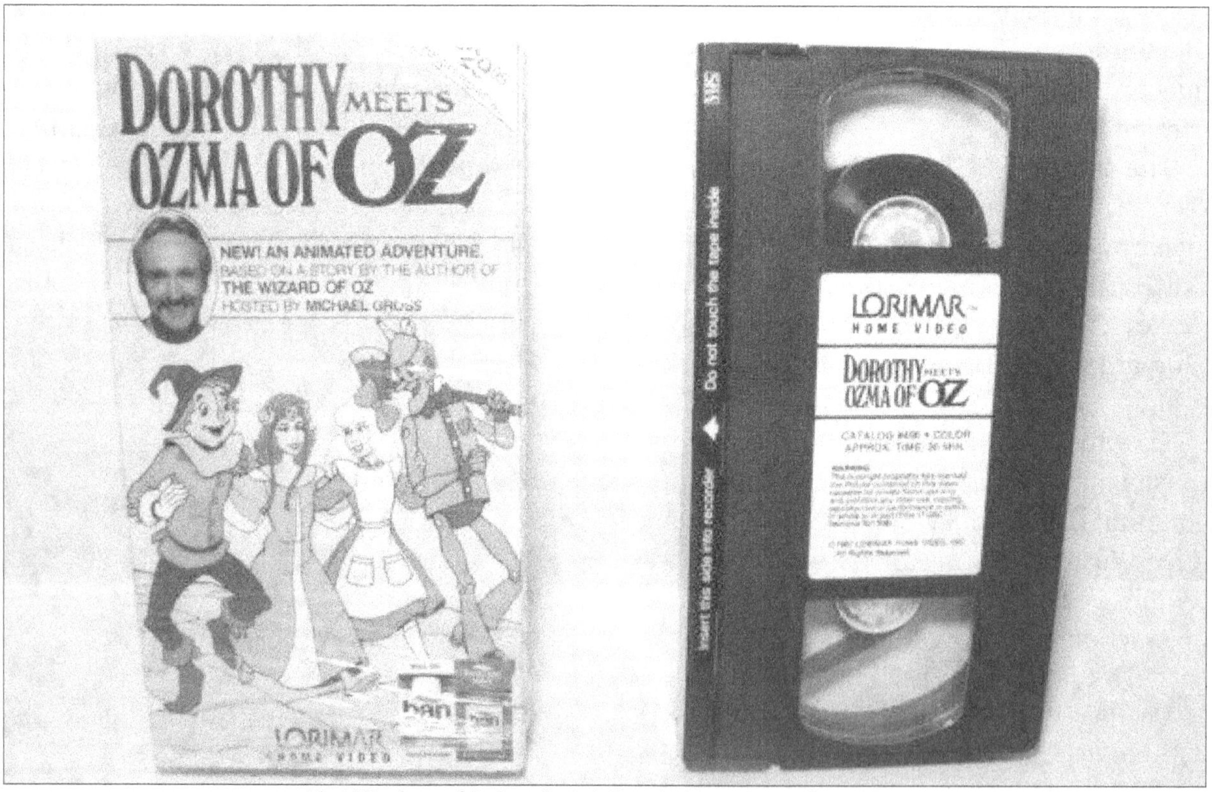

The VHS release of Kushner-Locke's *Dorothy Meets Ozma of Oz*, 1987.

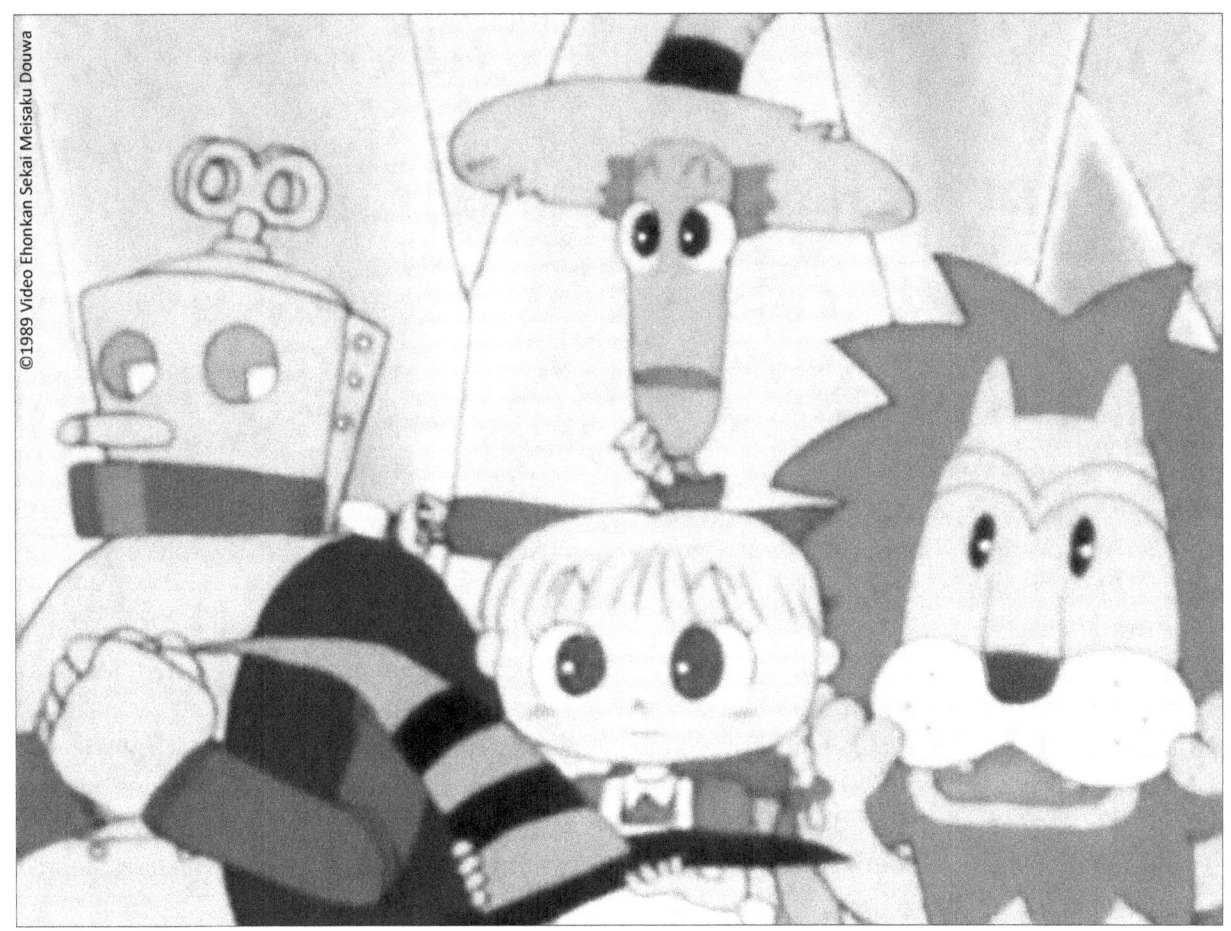

A scene from Funky Fable's *The Wizard of Oz*, released in 1989 by Video Ehonkan Sekai Meisaku Douwa.

Funky Fables / The Wizard of Oz (1989)

The Wizard of Oz is a colorful 1989 adaptation of the Lyman Frank Baum tale that appeared as part of the Japanese cartoon series, *Funky Fables*.

The program presented classic children's literary works in a chibi art style. Produced by Video Ehonkan Sekai Meisaku Douwa, the Oz episode was released in English by Saban Entertainment Inc. The *Funky Fables* series ran for 26 episodes from 1988-1990.

The cartoon tells a more traditional version of Oz and borrows many lines unique to the 1939 MGM classic movie starring Judy Garland. In fact, Dorothy, in the animated story says to the Wizard, "If you're the Wizard then I'm Judy Garland!"

Eric S. Rollman produced the anime presentation. The executive producer was Jerald E. Bergh. Barbara A. Oliver wrote the story, which was edited by Tony Oliver. The supervising producer was Winston Richard. Doug Parker served as voice director.

Previously Rollman had produced the animated series DIC Entertainment's *The Super Mario Brothers Super Show*, and Ruby-Spears' *Alvin and the Chipmunks*. Subsequently, he worked as executive producer of hundreds of Marvel cartoon series, such as

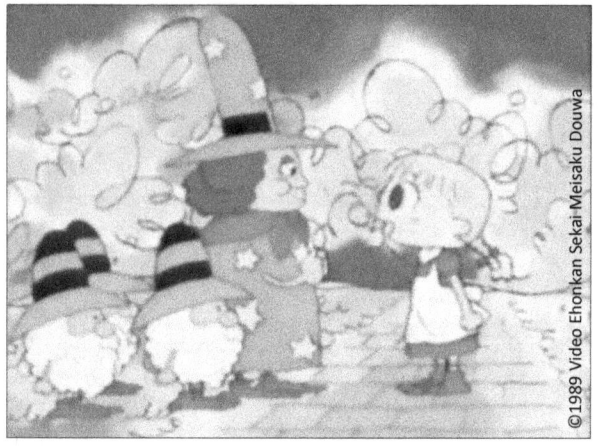

Dorothy meets the Good Witch and some Munchkins.

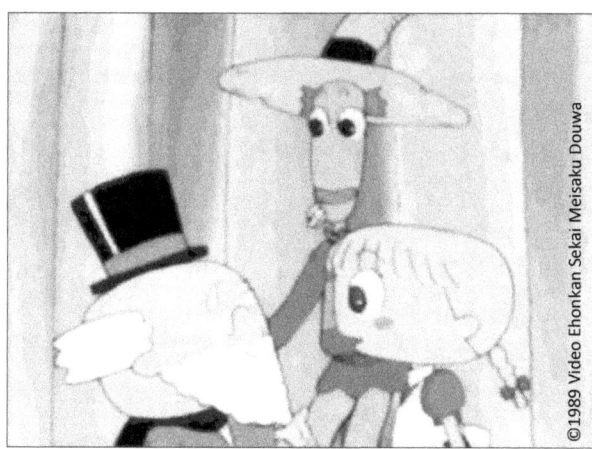

Dorothy and the Scarecrow speak with the Wizard.

The X-Men, Silver Surfer, The Incredible Hulk, The Avengers, The Spectacular Spider-Man, Black Panther, Fantastic Four, Iron Man, and more.

The English version features the talents of 11 individuals. The narrator of the program is Norma MacMillan. Character voices include Christine Lippa as Dorothy, Ian James Corlett as the Scarecrow, Britain Durham as the Tin Man, and Michael Donovan as the Lion. Doug Parker played the Wizard, with Barbara Whiting as the Wicked Witch of the West. Kate Robbins was Glinda, and Lee Tockar provided barks for Toto. The roles of Aunt Em and Uncle Henry are Cathy Weseluck and Scott McNeil.

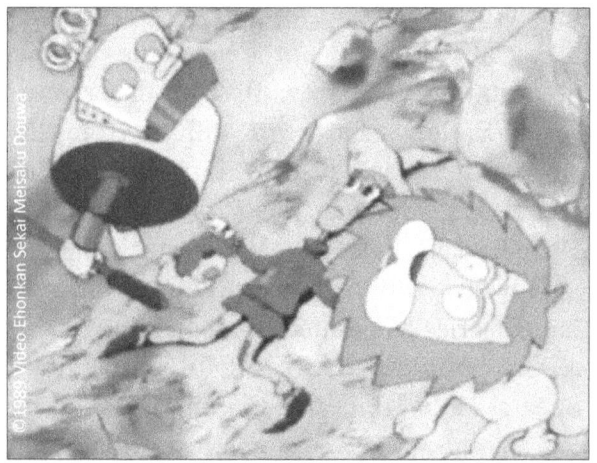

The Tin Man, Scarecrow and Cowardly Lion, after being attacked by flying monkeys.

The design of the main characters provides amusement. The Tin Man's body is in the shape of a facing-out drum. He also has a sizeable wind-up key on his head. The Cowardly Lion's mane is sharply pointed, lending anime style appeal. The Scarecrow is thin, and his tubular head topped with an oversized straw hat. The Wicked Witch resembles a hunch-backed hag. Half of Dorothy's small stature is her head, with big blue eyes, lending an adorable appearance.

The Wizard, Glinda, and the Munchkins are uninteresting visually, however the background art is scribbled and highlighted with bright, cheerful watercolors.

Many lines of dialogue from the cartoon have gained status among trivia buffs. Among them include the Tin Man saying in an Arnold Schwarzenegger tone, "It would take a man of steel to get into that place. Wait a minute. Tin is like steel. I'll become the Tinmanator!"

Tin Man also offers, "Without a heart, I can never really know what it would be like to love someone, or ever really understand trashy novels."

Dorothy says in one scene, "Well, we're not living in a trailer park, so we'll be alright."

The cartoon appears on YouTube.

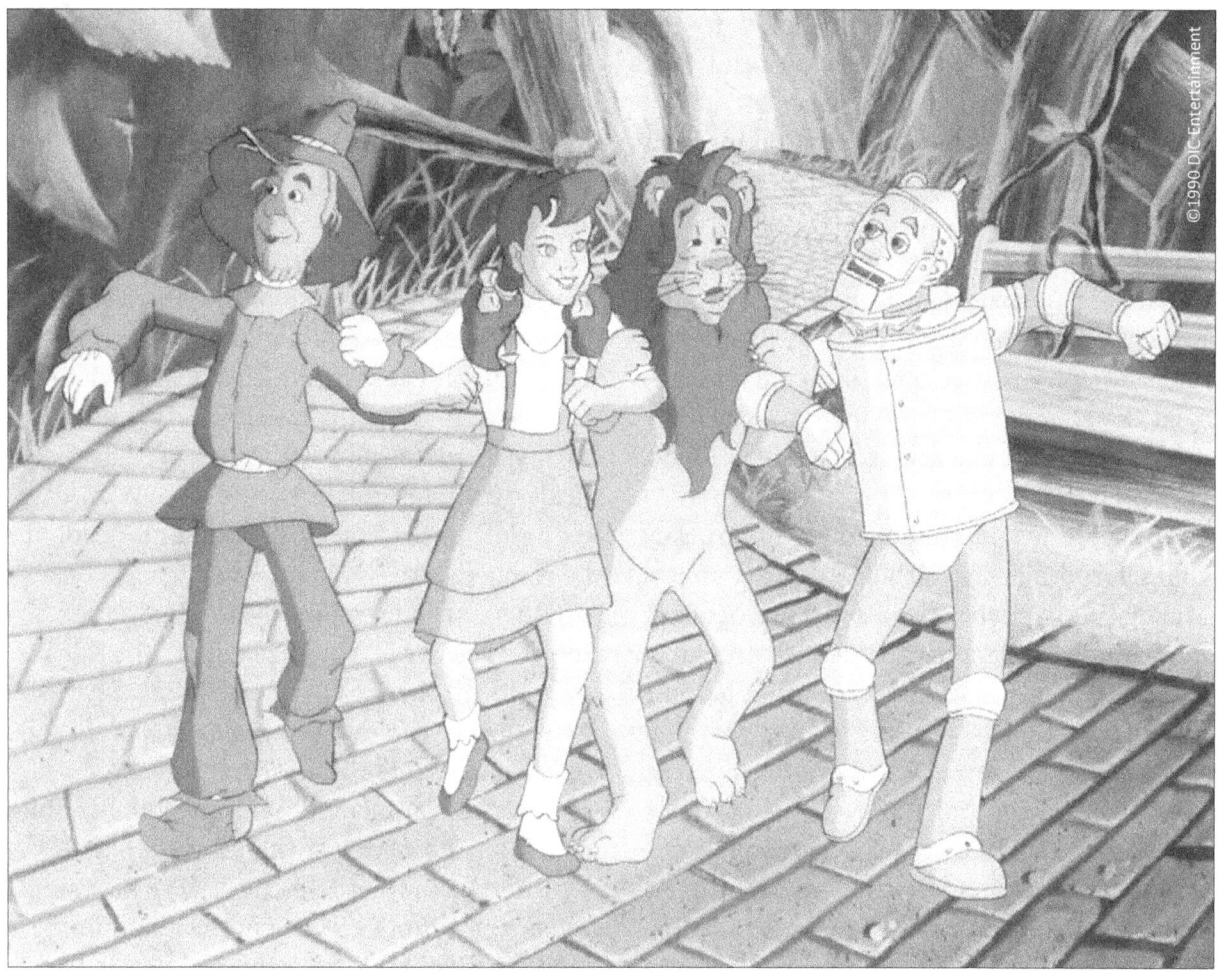

A scene from DIC's made-for-television series *The Wizard of Oz*, first broadcast Saturday mornings on ABC in 1990.

The Wizard of Oz (1990)

DIC Entertainment's *The Wizard of Oz*, a 1990 made-for-television cartoon, first appeared on September 8, 1990 on the ABC television network, Saturday mornings. Only 13 30-minute episodes were created. The series also aired on YTV in Canada, and Toon Disney presented reruns from 1998 to 2002.

The series, based on the debut Lyman Frank Baum book, *The Wonderful Wizard of Oz*, borrowed extensively from the 1939 MGM classic, due to Turner Entertainment's acquisition of the film. The DIC series was produced in conjunction with Turner.

In charge of production was Andy Heyward, Robby London, Michael Maliani, and John O'Sullivan Francis Jr.

In the series, Dorothy returns to Oz with Toto embarking on new adventures. All of her buddies are there, such as the Cowardly Lion, the Tin Man, the Scarecrow, Glinda, and others. Also, the Wicked Witch of the West has been resurrected and taken over as ruler of the Emerald City. Dorothy and her team must try to rescue The Wizard, who has been cast aloft in a hot air balloon, unable to land and restore his authority.

Over a dozen writers contributed to the series, but only two, Elana Lesser and Cliff Ruby, were involved in all 13 episodes.

The series' art director, Kurt Conner, was joined by staffers Winnie Chaffee, Thierry P. Laurin, Brian A. Miller, and Alexis Wallrich.

Eight storyboard artists were set to work in the art department, which included Timothy Burgard, Kurt and Brad Conner, Tom Nesbitt, and John Ahern. Nine individuals managed the sound end of production, which included Peter Tomaszewicz, Heather Elliott and Michael J. Cowan.

In the series' animation department, key character designers included Kurt Conner, Michael Diederich and Rogerio Nogueira. Background designers included Alvaro Arce, Gilbert Hung, Lisa Souza and Vladimir Spasojevic.

Music for the series was provided by Tom Worrall. A slightly altered version of *We're Off to See The Wizard* was included in the program. Other supervising, assistant and editing positions were filled by over two dozen individuals.

Talents brought aboard to provide voices included Charlie Adler as the Cowardly Lion, Liz Georges as Dorothy, David Lodge as the Scarecrow, Hal Rayle as the Tin Man, Tress MacNeille as the Wicked Witch, B. J. Ward as Glinda, and Alan Oppenheimer as The Wizard. Included in one episode is actor Pat Fraley, who subsequently gained notoriety for his voiceover work in *Teenage Mutant Ninja Turtles* productions.

The 13 episodes began with a two-part adventure title *The Rescue of the Emerald City*. The tale has Dorothy and Toto returning to Oz to unseat the resurrected Wicked Witch of the West from the throne she had stolen from The Wizard to rule Oz. Most of the series deals with this dilemma, as The Wizard is cast aloft in his hot air balloon and needs to be rescued, too.

Other episodes include storylines such as the Wicked Witch conjuring up a fake Kansas to lure Dorothy into a scheme to steal her ruby slippers. The evil witch also steals the Lion's courage and gives it to a hyena.

In one adventure the Wicked Witch is able to render the power of the ruby slippers useless, and in another tale erases Oz history and the memories of everyone in the kingdom.

In another tale, everything appears to be opposite than what it actually is, there's an adventure where the witch steals music from a village and Dorothy and her companions are determined to restore the melodies.

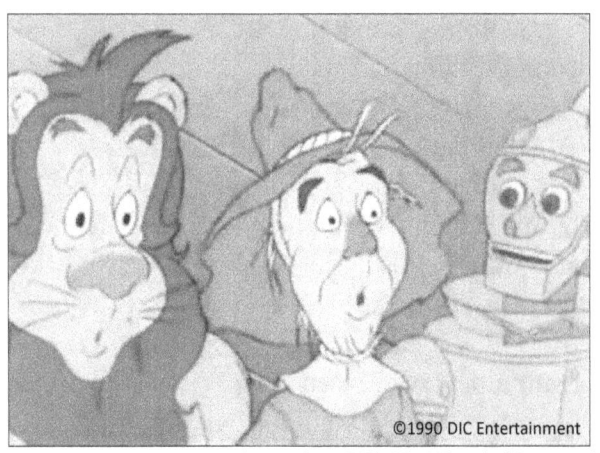 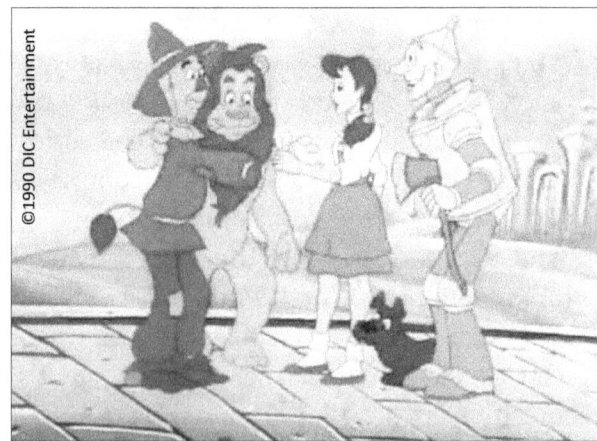

Scenes from DIC's *The Wizard of Oz*, a made-for-television series first broadcast in 1990.

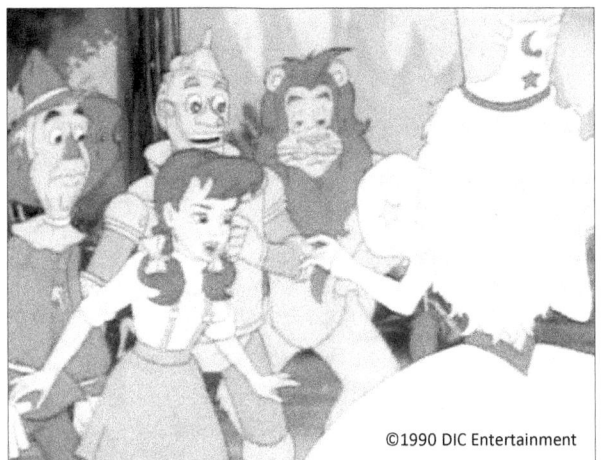
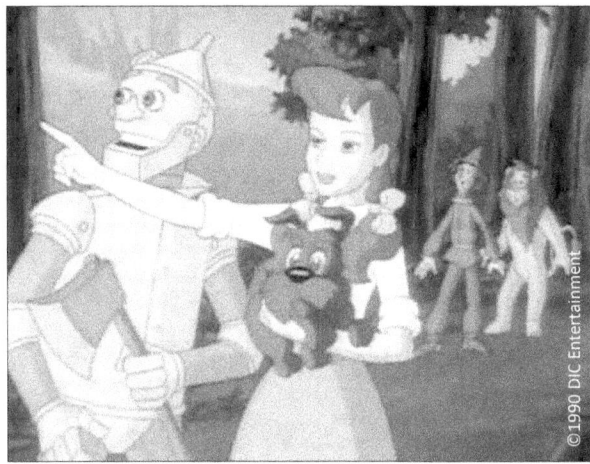

Scenes from DIC's *The Wizard of Oz*, a made-for-television series first broadcast in 1990.

An amusing adventure highlighting the Tin Man takes place in Mechanica, where everything is made out of tin.

The series was generally received unenthusiastically by young viewers who had seen enough of Oz animations that flooded the airwaves and home video markets in recent years. This likely was a reason why Turner didn't care for another season from DIC.

The quality of the cartoon is unremarkable leaving the series all but forgotten, even among Oz fans. Intended to be a continuation of the MGM classic, the series failed.

The final broadcast of the series on ABC took place on December 28, 1990. Selected episodes in the series were released in 1991, on VHS by Turner Home Entertainment. The UAV Corporation Station featured many episodes in a series of DVD's released from 2002-05.

The entire series has never been released in the United States on DVD. A non-English 4-disc collection did feature all episodes for the region of Serbia and Montenegro.

The Wizard of Oz Episode Guide

The Rescue of the Emerald City Part 1 / The Rescue of the Emerald City Part 2 / Fearless / Crystal Clear / We're Not in Kansas Anymore / The Lion that Squeaked / Dream a Little Dream / A Star is Gone / Time Town / The Marvelous Milkmaid of Mechanica / Upside-Down Town / The Day the Music Died / Hot Air.

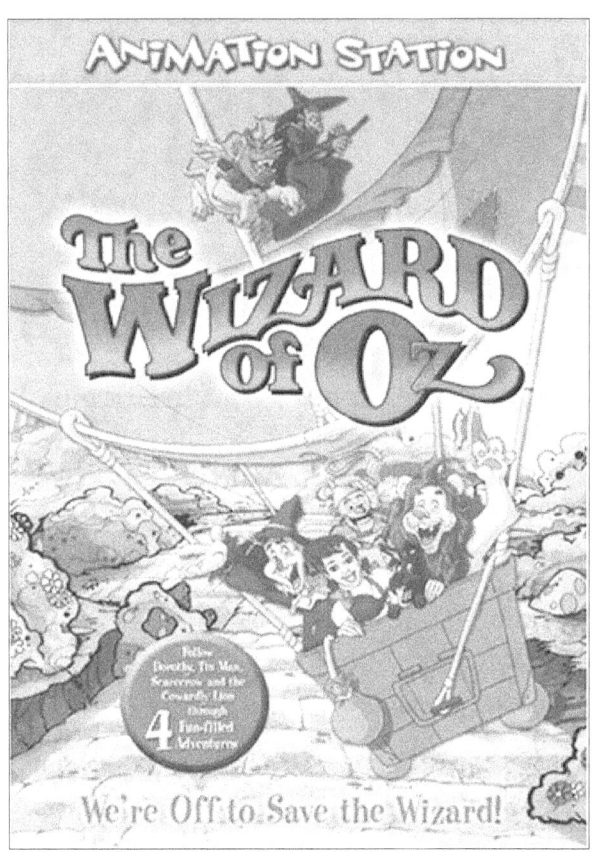

One of the UAV Corporation's *The Wizard of Oz* DVD volumes.

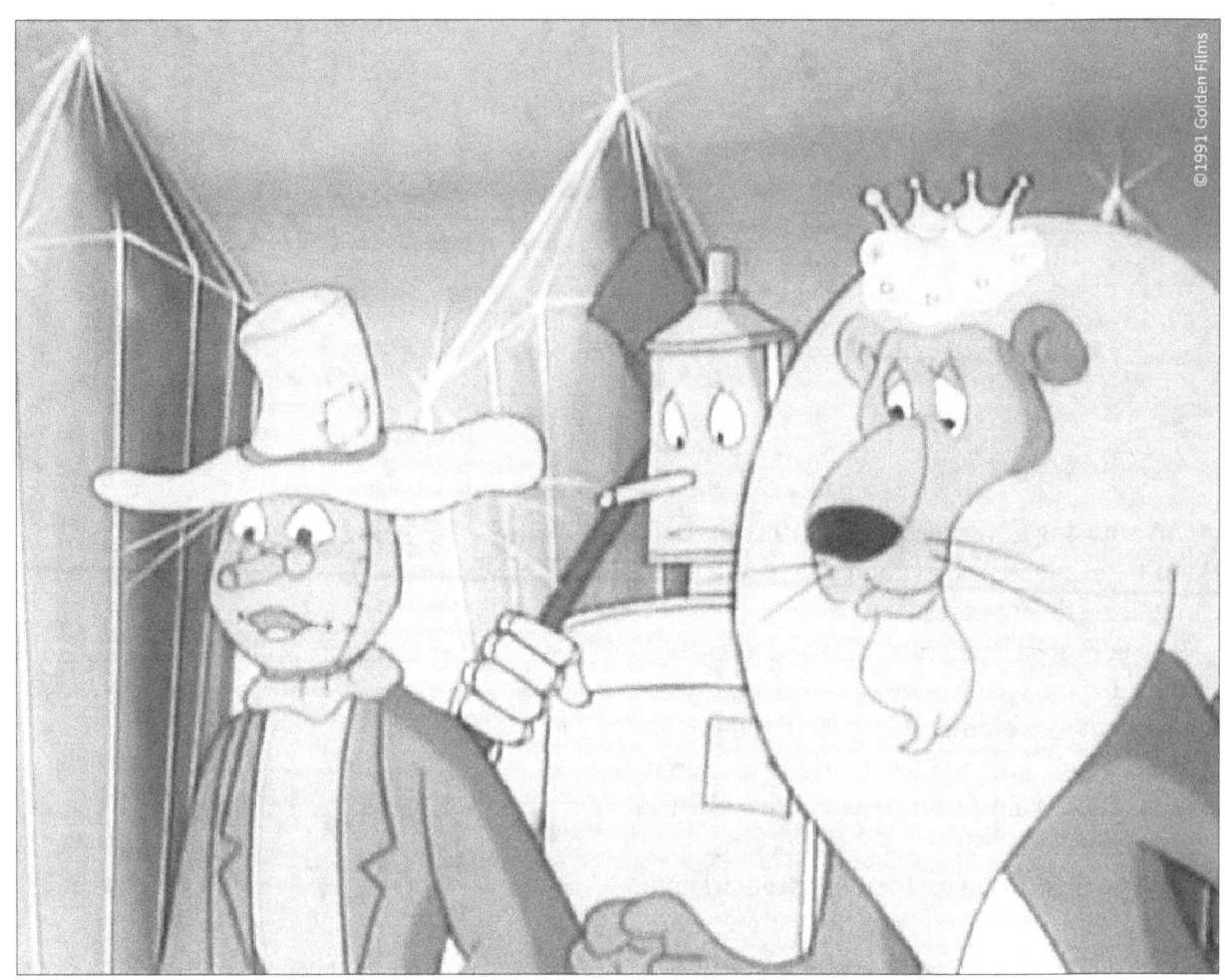

A scene from Golden Films' *The Wizard of Oz*, a direct-to-video 1991 release.

The Wizard of Oz (1991)

Golden Films' *The Wizard of Oz*, originating from South Korea, is a 25-minute cartoon released straight to video in 1991. The screenplay, written by Roger Scott Olsen, tells the traditional tale seen in Lyman Frank Baum's first Oz book, *The Wonderful Wizard of Oz*.

The production supervisor of the cartoon, Pico Hozumi, began his career in animation in 1977 with the release of *The Mouse and the Child*. He had worked on a previous Oz cartoon as production coordinator, *Dorothy in the Land of Oz*, released by Fred Wolf Films in 1980. Hozumi is perhaps best known for being a production liaison in 1988 for DIC Entertainment's *The Real Ghostbusters* animated television series.

The cartoon was produced by Diane Eskenazi and Ron Layton, with Jim Simon serving as co-producer.

Eskenazi gained recognition and awards for producing over 80 children's films. Layton was known for his work supervising animated direct-to-video cartoons for Golden Films such as *Thumbelina, Pinocchio, Beauty and the Beast, Sleeping Beauty, Jack and the Beanstalk, Cinderella,* and *The Jungle*

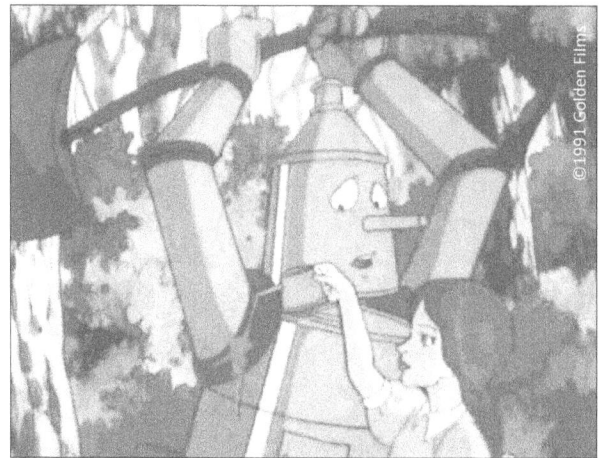 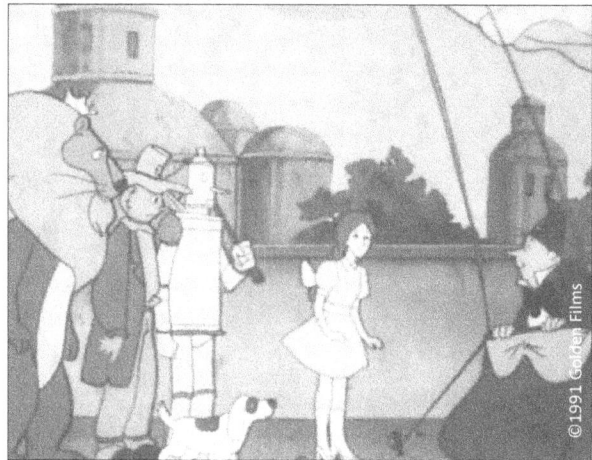

Dorothy oils the Tim Man, and speaks to The Wizard in his hot air balloon, in scenes from Golden Films' *The Wizard of Oz*, 1991.

Book, among others.

Critics viewed Layton's works as cheap knock-off's of superior Disney feature films.

Providing the primary voices in Golden Films' *The Wizard of Oz* was Jim Cummings and Terri Hawkes.

Cummings' voiceover resume in animation is enormous, appearing in Disney productions, Hanna Barbera cartoons, *Spider-Man*, *Star Wars*, *Transformers*, *Curious George*, *Looney Tunes*, and more.

Hawkes subsequently provided voiceovers for many projects, including a series of *Care Bears* productions.

The short animated cartoon follows the creations and situations found in Lyman Frank Baum's book, *The Wonderful Wizard of Oz*, with little exception. It's not based on the MGM picture, unlike other animated productions that produced hybrids.

One unusual twist is that the Scarecrow wears a pair of eyeglasses.

The downside of the cartoon is the animation is unsmooth in motion and sometimes jumpy. At times, characters appear to be out of scale and proportion to their counterparts.

Modeling for certain characters, such as Dorothy and The Wizard, failed to create appealing and likable appearances. At times, Dorothy resembles a lifeless mannequin, and The Wizard looks like a total creeper that you would keep children a safe distance from.

Some of the characters, such as the Scarecrow and Lion, don't appear to possess what they are seeking all along. Examples of the Scarecrow using his smarts, or the Lion showing moments of bravery, are strangely missing.

The cartoon was released on VHS home video for a period, then Goodtimes Video released it on DVD in 2004, branding it one in a series of Golden Films' "Collectible Classics."

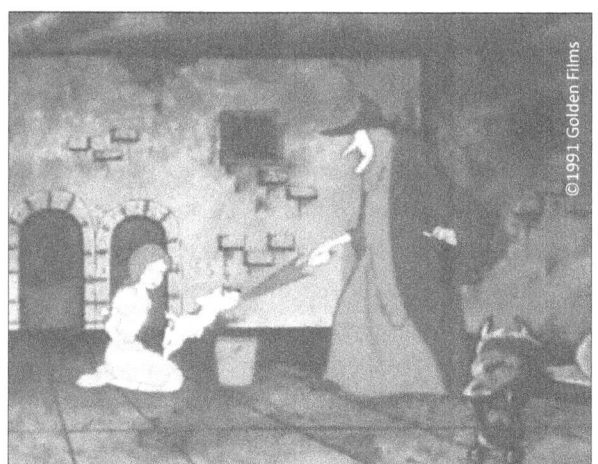

Dorothy encounters the Wicked Witch in *The Wizard of Oz*, 1991.

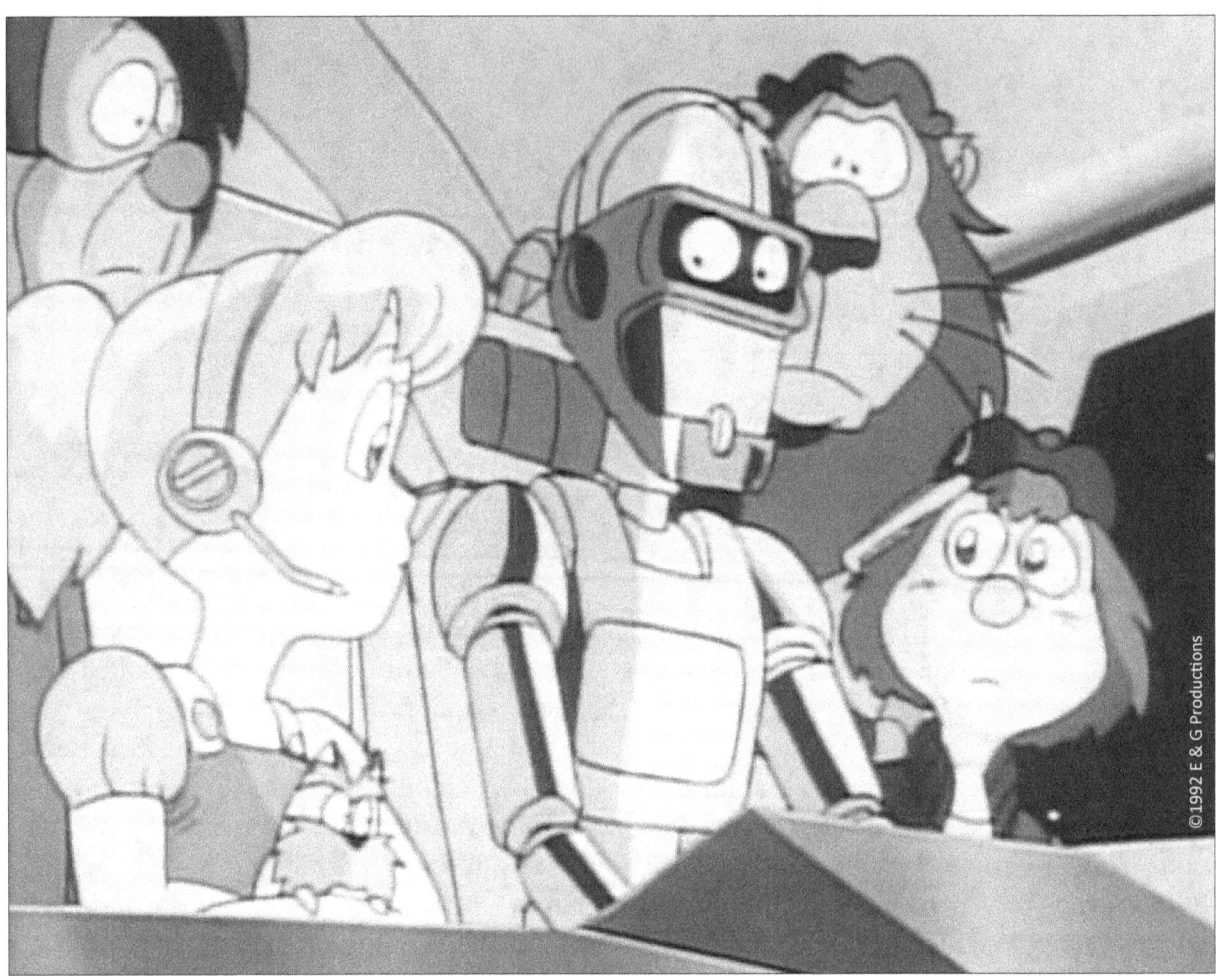

Chopper pilots the spacecraft in a scene from *The Wonderful Galaxy of Oz*, released in 1992 by E & G Productions.

The Wonderful Galaxy of Oz (1992)

The Wonderful Galaxy of Oz is a sci-fi Japanese anime television series that puts a futuristic spin on the classic Lyman Frank Baum original. Produced by Enoki Films, TX Network, and E&G Productions, the cartoon blasted off October 5, 1992, on Japan television. The show, initially titled *Space Oz no Bōken* (*Adventures of Space Oz*), ran for 26 episodes, concluding on April 4, 1993.

Shortly after the program's run on Japanese TV, Enoki Films edited the premiere episode of the series with parts from subsequent episodes into a feature-length movie, featuring English language translation. It was available in the United States on VHS tape then DVD.

The series, set in the year 2060, begins with a crisis. Three suns have converged in the sky, creating a catastrophic event on Earth that only occurs every 1,000 years. The alignment creates storms and earthquakes, but with the epicenter being Kansas. Uncle Henry, from his computer headquarters in his rustic home, phones Dorothy, alerting her, and ordering her to come home.

However, when she arrives home, Toto

gets loose and finds safety inside her uncle's spacecraft on the property. She follows the dog into the ship.

Chopper, her uncle's robot assistant, tails Dorothy into the craft, urging her to follow him to the shelter. Chopper is a techy version of the Tin Man. He's a robot who borrows some of his appearance from *Star Wars'* C3-PO and even has his accent, too.

However, Chopper's arrival comes too late, as a tornado is rapidly approaching.

Henry tells Dorothy, via a wireless headset, that she must take to the controls of the ship and blast off into space until the storm subsides. Then, she can return home. She complies and blasts off.

But a twister of another kind awaits, a black hole in space.

Dorothy, Toto, and Chopper hold on as the black hole sucks them in, and deposits them into another galaxy. Upon exiting, the group finds themselves in an alien space battle with an alien spacecraft. Their ship is disabled, and lands on a planet called Oz.

Dorothy and her companions first meet Plantman, who enters their craft upon arrival. Plantman is an alien equivalent of the Scarecrow. While the original was made of

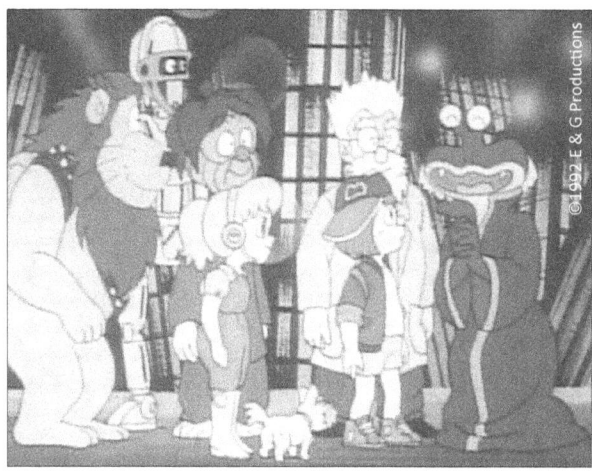

A scene from *The Wonderful Galaxy of Oz*, Doctor Oz, center.

fabric and stuffed with hay, this creature is an organic, living, and talking plant. He mimics the Scarecrow's floppy walk and posture.

Plantman fiddles with controls in the ship, causing an explosion. The four exit just in time, but now the little girl has no way of returning home.

Fortunately, Dorothy's dune buggy, which was in the craft, is blown free and unscathed. They use it to journey to see the Wizard. He wants a brain, Dorothy wants a new ship.

On their way to Oz, they befriend a cowardly lion named Lionman, who displays the posture of an ape. He tags along. Perhaps the Wizard can give him some courage.

Chopper joins the wish list, imagining the Wizard might provide him with a heart.

They encounter many obstacles, like an enormous robotic dragon, commanded by Gloomhilda. She's the Wicked Witch upgrade, evil and loud-mouthed. But the foursome defeats her and the army of Skeezers she controls.

The victory doesn't go unnoticed by the keepers of Oz, as a party arrives in a dirigible welcoming them aboard.

The airship takes them to Oz. It's a city beneath a dome, floating in the sky. The citizens

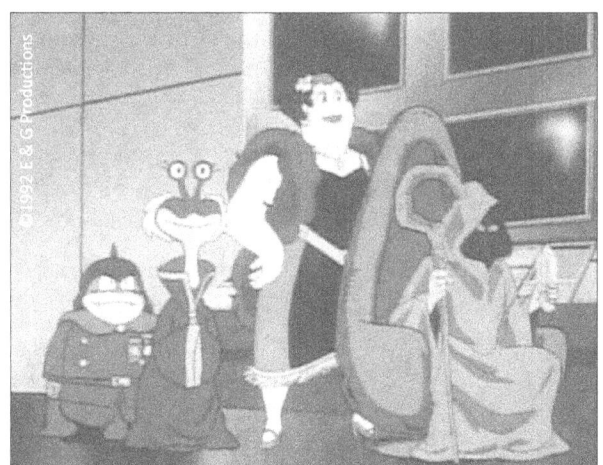

A scene from *The Wonderful Galaxy of Oz*, Gloomhilda, center.

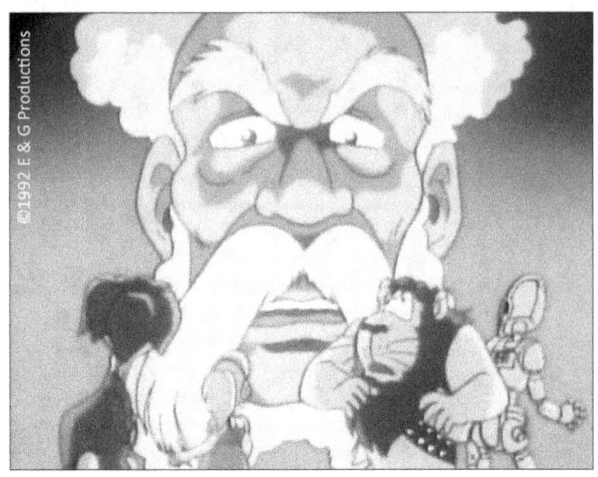

A scene from *The Wonderful Galaxy of Oz*, The Wizard, middle.

celebrate their arrival with open arms, recognizing Dorothy and her companions defeated Gloomhilda.

The visitors are granted a meeting with the Wizard. A large head and free-floating hands represent the Wizard they encounter. But something is suspiciously wrong. In short order, they discover a boy named Mosey is operating the mechanical illusion.

Mosey's father is the real Wizard, known as Doctor Oz, who appears to them in a hologram encouraging the team to go on an interstellar mission to save Oz. They must find three magic crystals, which are spread across the universe before they fall into the hands of Gloomhilda.

Mosey offers his father's spacecraft, named The Rainbow Road, to embark on the mission. He joins Dorothy, Toto, Chopper, Plantman, and Lionman aboard the craft, and off they go.

The team encounters many creatures, both good and evil, and is in constant danger from Gloomhilda and her minions. It's a Star Wars adventure gone Oz. In the cockpit of the ship together, Chopper and Lionman remind you of C3-PO and Chewbacca.

Part of their motivation as a reward for saving the planet of Oz, all might be granted their wishes, including Dorothy's hope to return home to Kansas.

The group trades humorous insults during the series. Examples are Lionman calling Plantman "cabbage head," and Plantman calls young Mosey a "rug rat."

Spaceflight, crafts, and the technology on display visually fall somewhere in between the TV cartoon series *Robotech* and *Galaxy High School*.

A large cast provided character voices for the series. Mariko Kouda provided the voice of Dorothy. Hiroshi Takemura played Chopper. Noriko Kamimura played Gloomhilda. Ai Satou played Emily Obasan, and Hagi. Eken Mine played the Minister, and Virtual President. Hidetoshi Nakamura played Yabor. Hirohiko Kakegawa played Bisuti. Ichiro Murakoshi played Doctor Oz, Moji's Father. Katsumi Suzuki played the General of Oz, and Toto. Kazuhiko Kishino played Santa. Kazuo Oka played Henry Ojisan, Paul's Father. Kenichi Ono played Jill. Kozo Shioya played Plante. Kumiko Nishihara played Azuma. Kumiko Takizawa played the Queen. Mahito Tsujimura played Rakudo. Mami Matsui played Moji. Mari Adachi played the

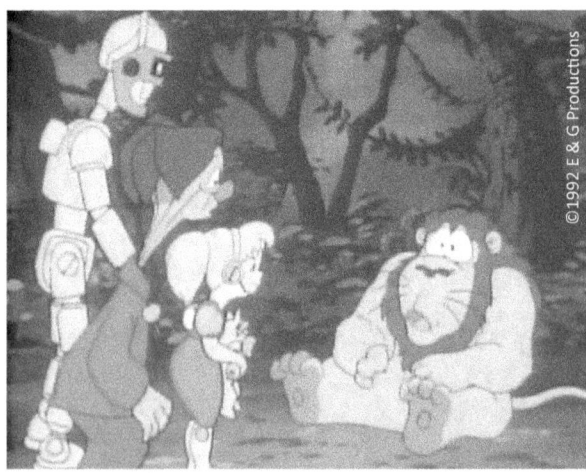

A scene from *The Wonderful Galaxy of Oz*, meeting the Lion.

52

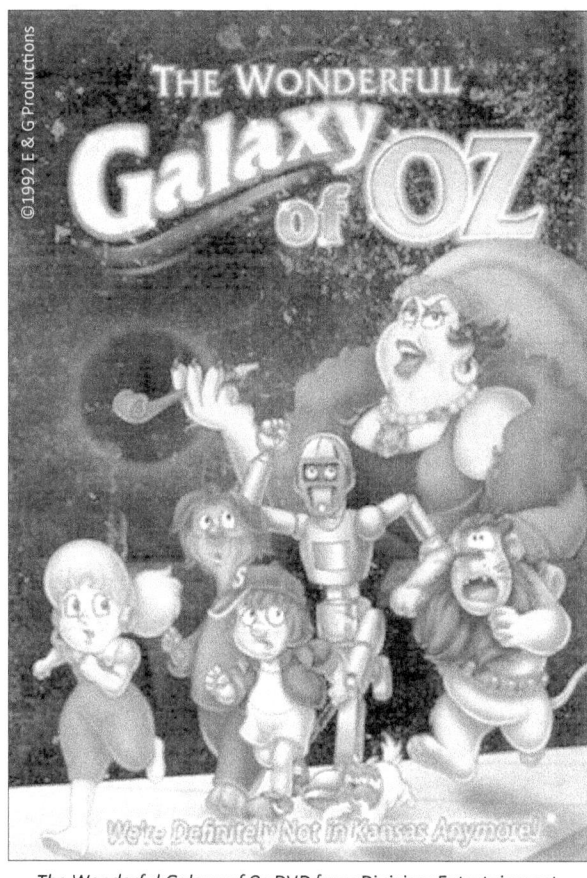

The Wonderful Galaxy of Oz DVD from Digiview Entertainment.

Koras Girl, and Maid. Mariko Ikegami played Nicholas. Miki Narahashi played Misha's Mother. Minoru Inaba played Alherihit. Mitsuo Chida played Robot A. Miyuki Matsushita played Rabbit, and Sister. Narumi Hidaka played Teddy Bear. Natsumi Sakuma played the Witch of the West. Reiko Suzuki played Mother. Rica Matsumoto played the Baby Dinosaur. Ryuuzou Ishino played Hunter, and the Radio Voice. Satomi Koorogi played Misha. Shinobu Adachi played Toma. Shinpachi Tsuji played Baresuku, the Captain, and Hunter. Shōzō Iizuka played Oz. Takumi Yamazaki played Adjutant, Soldier A, and Stag. Toshiyuki Morikawa played Athletic. Yasuo Muramatsu plays the King. Yuri Amano played Princess Shera. Yuri Shiratori played Lily. And last but not least, Yuuichi Nagashima also played Hunter.

The original Japanese version of the series identified the wicked witch as "Glumilda."

The Wonderful Galaxy of Oz is available on DVD from Digiview Entertainment. However, it's not the entire series, but rather an edited down, 75-minute movie dubbed in English.

The series was unique, funny, and always entertaining. It is one of most imaginative Oz cartoons ever produced. Perhaps one day the 26 episodes will be released in the United States on DVD in their original Japanese language form, with English subtitles.

The Wonderful Galaxy of Oz Episode Guide

Dorothy Wanders into the World of Oz / The Surprising Secret of the King of Oz / Mystery of the Crystal Empire / The World's Cowardly Hero / The Sleeping Beauty of Mangabu / Chopper's Heart / Entrust Fasion to Me / Baby-Sitter Crisis / The Promise with Rockman Yabor / Scrapia of Scrapper / Grand Prix of Planet Car / Dorothy's Santa Claus / Chopper's Lover / Escape from Planet Game / Horror Birthday / Planet Water Rescue Mission / War of the Toy Country / Monster Panic / Crowded Amusement Park / The Plant Which Papa and I Defend / Legend of Captain Garo / Return to the Alherhit Hometown / Film Star Gloomhilda / The Reunion with Doctor Oz / The Return of the Witch from the West / Miracle of the Rainbow Crystal.

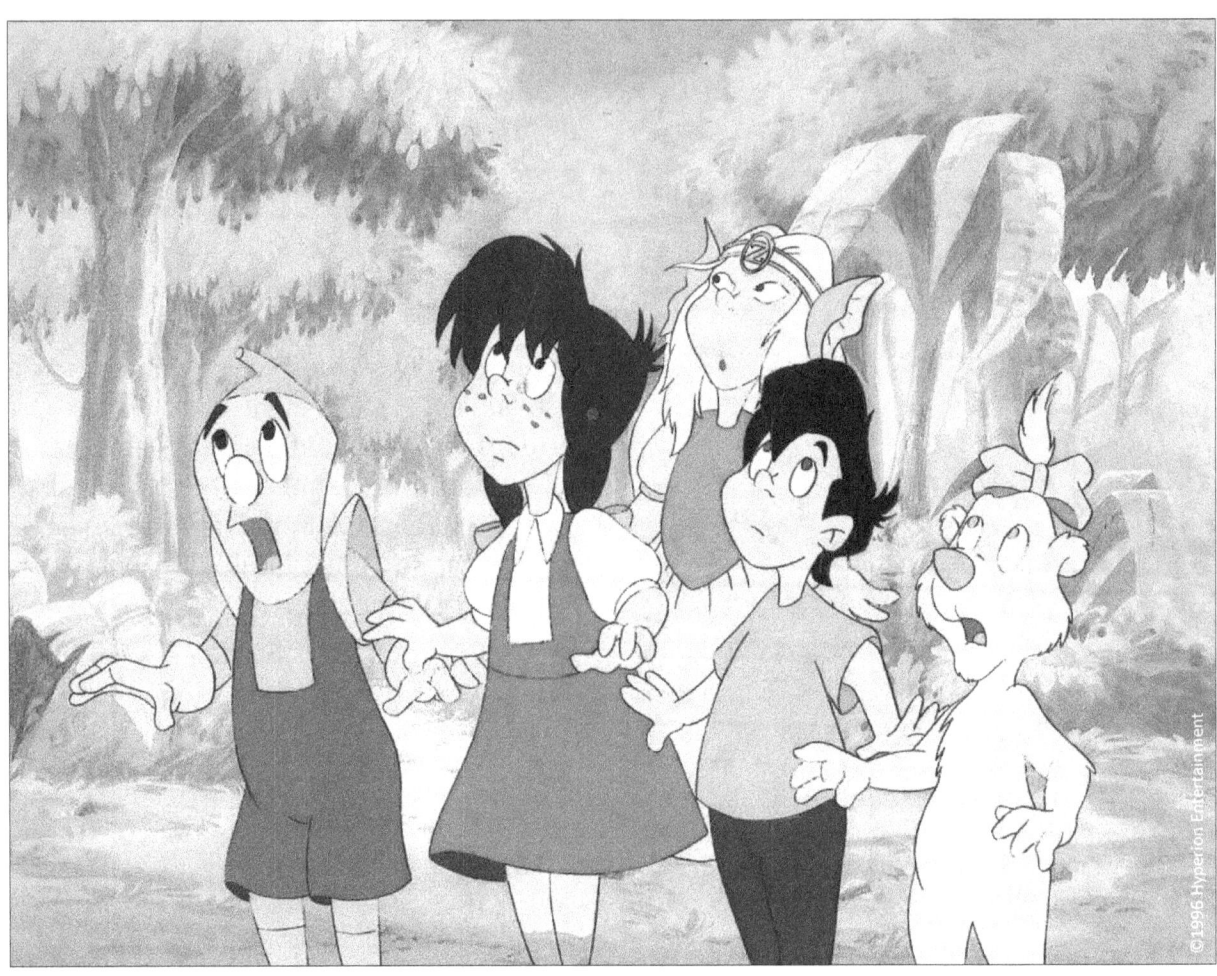

A scene from Hyperion's *The Oz Kids* animated television series, 1996.

The Oz Kids (1996)

The Oz Kids is an animated television series, produced by Hyperion Animation, that made its debut on the ABC network on September 14, 1996. The 26-episode adaptation of *Oz* featured two main characters, Dot and Neddie, both children of the adult Dorothy (Gale) and her husband, Zeb Hugson.

The show featured the juvenile offspring of familiar Oz characters, such as the Lion's kids Boris and Bela, the Tin Man's son Tinboy, Scarecrow Jr., Jack Pumpkinhead Jr., the Wizard's son Frank, and Glinda's daughter Andrea.

The program borrowed from a popular theme at the time, such as the *Muppet Babies*, where child versions of adult characters comprise a cast.

Dot, age 8, and Neddie, age 5, live in a Kansas farmhouse and they have a pet dog named Toto.

Other kid Oz characters popped in and out of the series, including the daughter of the Patchwork Girl.

The primary adversaries in the show were Mombi, and Otto, the son of the Nome King.

The Oz Kids was directed by Thomas E.

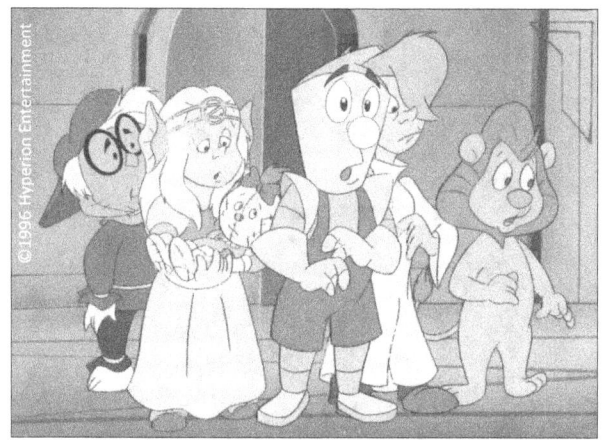 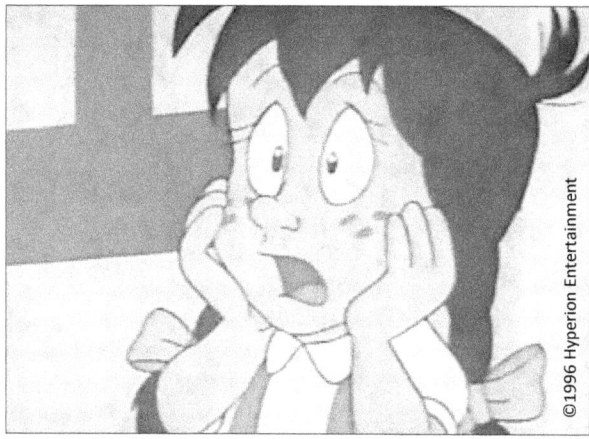

Scenes from Hyperion's *The Oz Kids,* presenting the children of favorite Oz characters.

Decker, Bert King, Rhoydon Shishido and David Teague. All four men also created storyboards. In charge of animation were Travis Cowsill and Mercedes J. Sichon.

Cowsill later worked on *Timon & Pumbaa, Ed, Edd 'n' Eddy*, and *The Toad Patrol*.

Sichon subsequently worked on *The Adventures of Hyperman, Loonatics Unleashed, Shaggy and Scooby-Doo Get a Clue*, and *Back at the Barnyard*.

Providing voices for the series were Erika Schickel as Dorothy, and Ross Maplettoft as her husband, Zeb. The voices for featured characters included Shay Astar, Julianne Michelle, Bradley Pierce, Benjamin Salisbury, Jonathan Taylor Thomas, Andy Milder, Steve Stoliar, Lawrence Tierney, and Aaron Michael Metchik, among others. Billy Mumy, of *Lost in Space*, did the voice of Sam.

The adventures centered around crisis, something bad has gone down, and the kids come to the rescue.

One episode takes place in the city of New York, while others originate in the land of Oz. Another story places the kids in China.

In one adventure Prince Otto discovers the Nome King's underground tunnel system beneath the Emerald City, and the kids end up underground again in another tale on a wild bus ride.

Santa is kidnapped in one adventure, while another tale has the kids encountering mermaids and sea devils when the boat they are aboard sinks.

In much of the series, computers and technology is used to transport the children to various locations.

Many of the characters depicted as children are cute, but some resemble any other toon animal or kid found on Saturday mornings at the time. Tinboy is particularly simple, without much distinctive in design.

While the series is fun, there's nothing original or remarkable about it. The animation is standard TV-style, and the background art, while colorful, is often bland.

Paramount released many episodes in the series as collections on VHS videotape. The series has not be issued on DVD, probably due to lack of interest.

The Oz Kids
Partial Episode Guide

Toto Lost in New York / The Monkey Prince / Journey Beneath the Sea / Christmas in Oz / The Return of Mombi / The Gnome Prince and the Magic Belt / Who Stole Santa? / Underground Adventure / Virtual Oz.

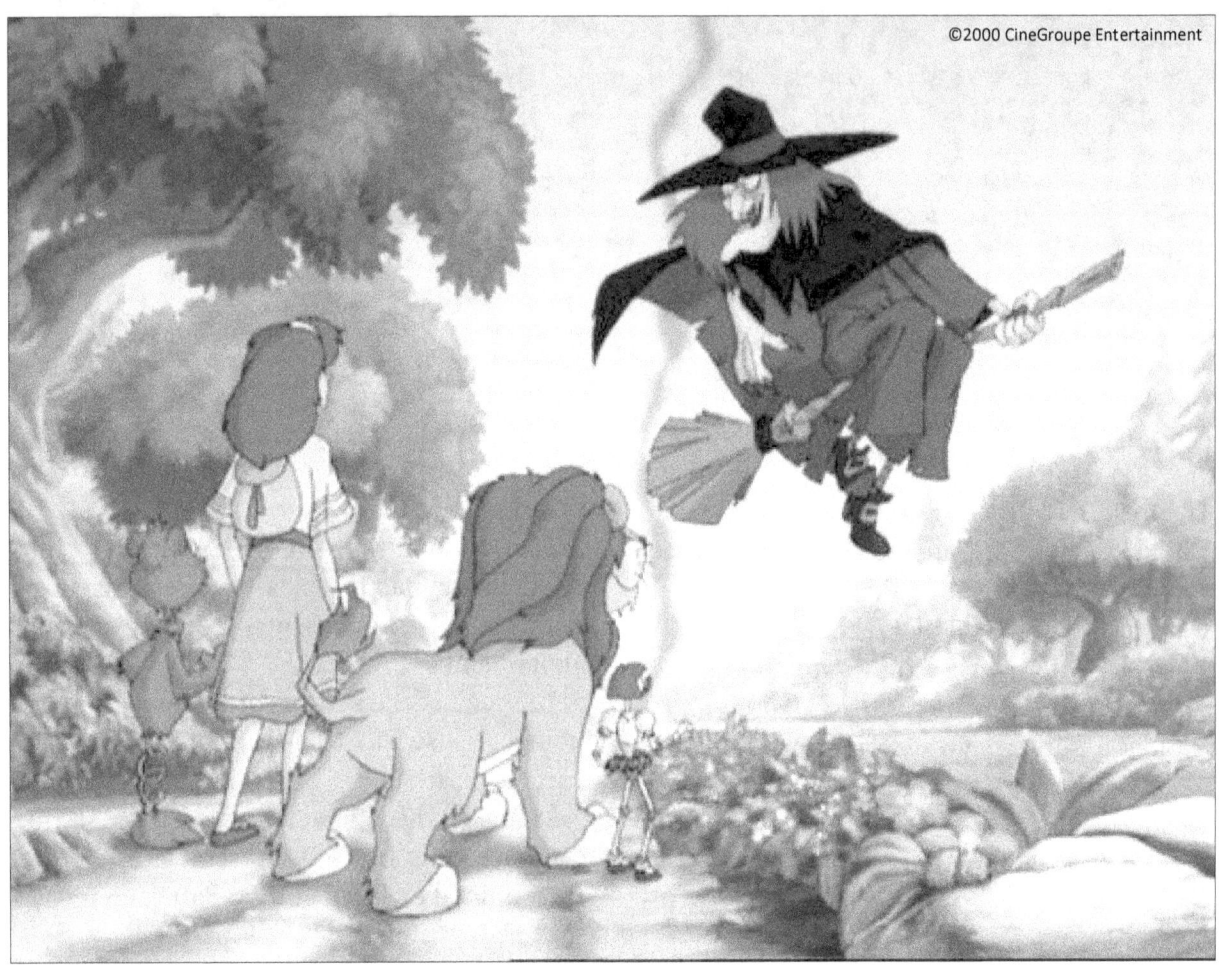

In a scene from the 2000 CineGroupe animated feature, *The Lion of Oz*, Wimzik and the Lion confront the Wicked Witch of the East.

The Lion of Oz (2000)

The Lion of Oz is a feature-length animated movie produced by CineGroupe, distributed by Lions Gates Films, for the Disney Channel. It debuted on September 26, 2000.

The 74-minutes film features a story that supposedly took place before Baum's first book, *The Wonderful Wizard of Oz*.

The screenplay, written by Elana Lesser and Cliff Ruby, is based on the book *Lion of Oz and the Badge of Courage*, by Roger S. Baum, the great-grandson of the originator.

The film was produced by Sophie Chicoine, Loris Kramer Lunsford, Michel Lemire and Jacques Pettigrew. It was directed by Tim Deacon. Music for the movie was composed by Jennifer Wilson.

Voices for characters were provided by several recognized talents, such as Dom DeLuise as circus balloonist Oscar Diggs, Jason Priestley as the Lion, Lynn Redgrave as the Wicked Witch of the East, and Bobcat Goldthwait as Silly Ozbul. Supporting character voices were performed by Tim Curry, Kathy Griffin, and others. Henry Beckman served as story narrator.

Art department personnel included Errol

Burke, Ghislain Barbe, James Caswell, Ihor Czeryba, Barry Jack, Velislav Kazakov, Isabelle Lamoureux, Joshua Lee, Craig Wilson, and Gregory Woronchak.

Ninety-four talents worked on the animation for *The Lion of Oz*, which included Ronaldo Roel Beltran, Errol Burke, Nadja Cozic, Lito De Mondo, Valerie Fontaine, Joshua Lee, and Hugo Lee, to name a few.

Five individuals were assigned to sound management, with eight providing the movie's special effects.

The story centers around the Cowardly Lion, who was formally a caged attraction with the traveling Omaha Circus. His one true pal is Oscar Diggs, a balloonist.

The Lion is awarded a badge of courage for ascending with Diggs in his hot air balloon, but the two are swept up in a storm that carries them to Oz.

There's plenty to see in this quality feature, such as living/talking trees, a springing teddy bear, a toy soldier named Captain Fitzgerald, and some fairies.

The Wicked Witch of the East spreads her evil across the land, with her henchmen and a sidekick named Gloom at her beck and call.

Many friends join the Lion during his trav-

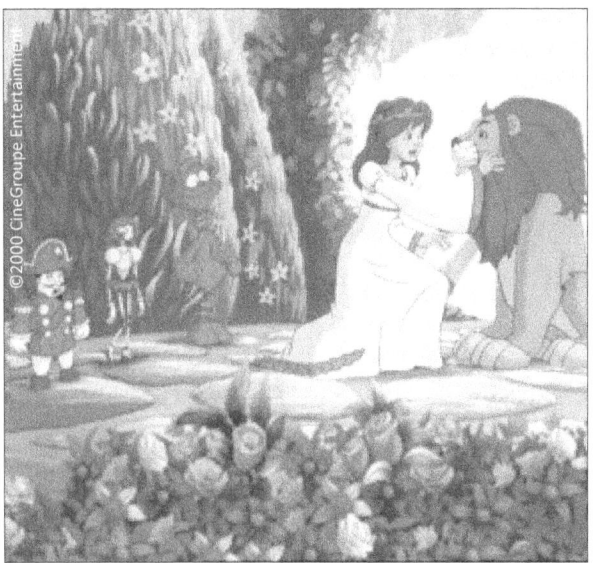

A scene from CineGroupe's *The Lion of Oz*.

els, including a character named Wimzik, who resembles Dorothy. She has a connection to the mystical Flower of Oz.

When Diggs turns up missing, the evil witch coveys she abducted him and holds him prisoner in her castle. If the Lion wants to see his pal again, he must find the Flower of Oz and bring it to her. Without the flower, the Witch cannot obtain rule over Oz.

The Lion discovers Diggs was never her prisoner, it was only a ploy. The witch steals the Lion's badge, robbing him of his courage, but that cannot stop Wimzik. Harnessing some flower power, Wimzik banishes the witch and assumes the throne.

The "cowardly" Lion bids his friends a sorrowful farewell. His journey ahead leads him to a yellow brick road. In the last scene of the movie, he meets Dorothy, the Tin Man, and the Scarecrow. It is the precise moment the Lion first appears in Lyman Frank Baum's *The Wonderful Wizard of Oz* book.

The film is entertaining, well written, and attractive artistically.

Sony Wonder Video released a DVD in 2000. It is also available from itunes.

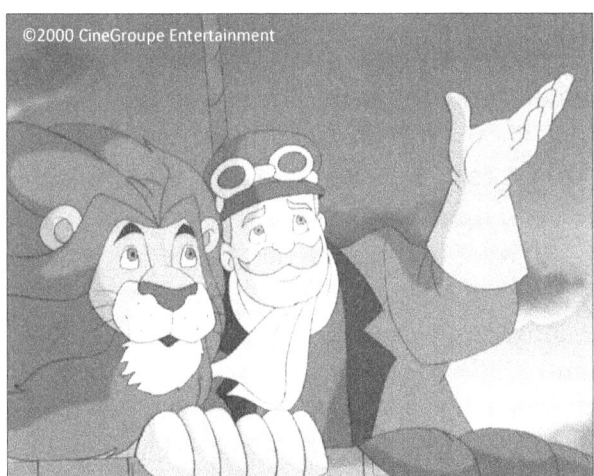

A scene from CineGroupe's *The Lion of Oz*.

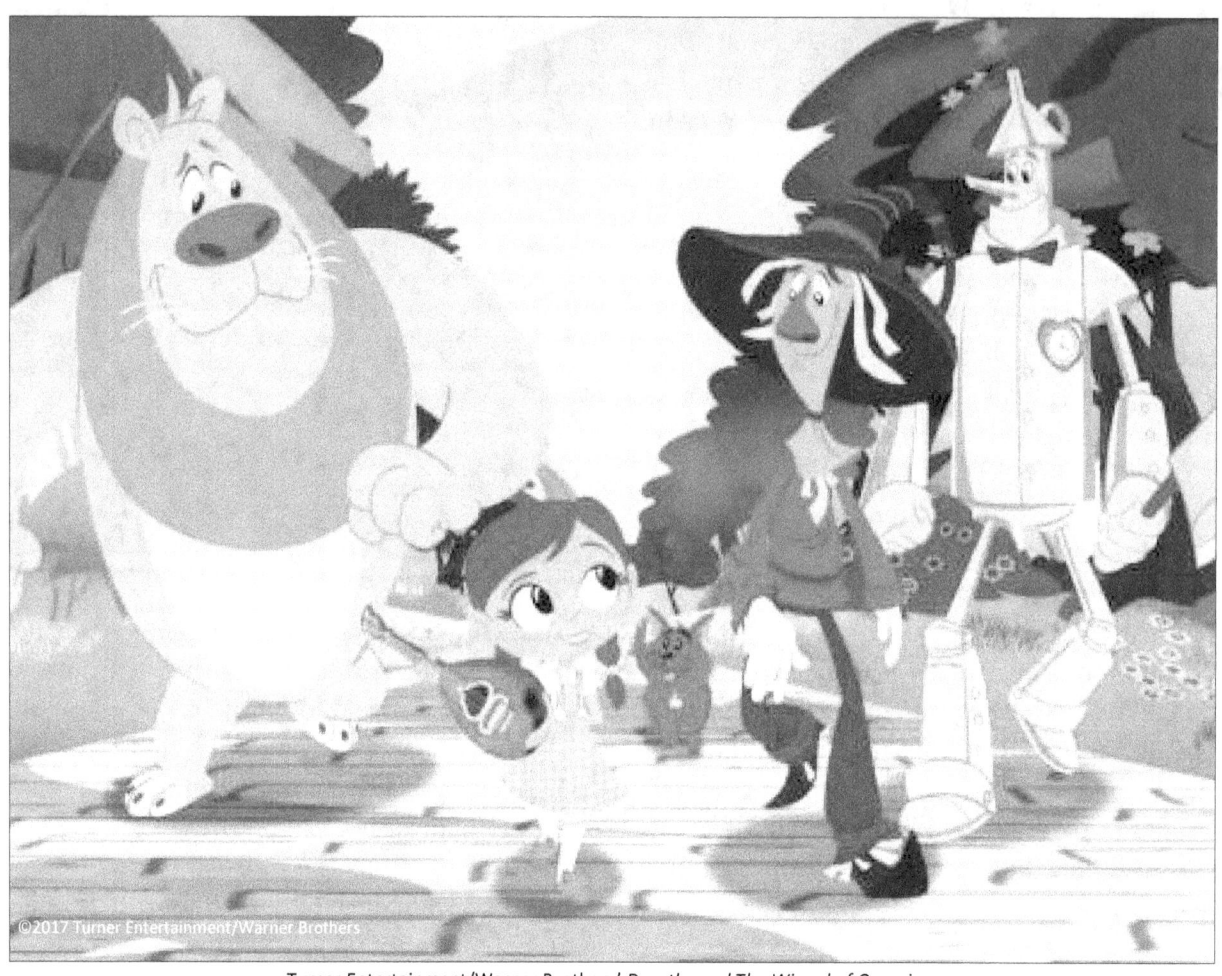

Turner Entertainment/Warner Brothers' *Dorothy and The Wizard of Oz* series.

Dorothy and The Wizard of Oz (2017)

Dorothy and The Wizard of Oz is an animated television series that made its debut on June 29, 2017, on Boomerang streaming video on demand. It is produced by Turner Entertainment Company, distributed by Warner Brothers Television.

The 22-minute cartoons are based on the books written by Lyman Frank Baum and the 1939 MGM live-action classic film, starring Judy Garland. Each of the 25 episodes, with the exception of two, present two stories.

Serving as producers on the series are Jay Bastian, Jeff DeGrandis, Michelle Jabloner-Weiss, Adam Middleton, Leanne Moreau, Sam Register, and Tony Salama. Writers include Jeremy Adams, Nina G. Bargiel, Caroline Farah, Shea Fontana, and Hugh Webber. Directors include Kuni Tomita, Charles Visser, and Kexx Singleton.

Artists on the series include Narina Sokolova, Haley Muraki, William Terrel, Elsa Garagarza, Norma Klingler, Edemer Santos, and Will Terrell.

Character designers include Kirk Millett, Debra Armstrong, and Daniel Schier, among others. Peter Slattery serves as animation director, with Graham Tormey as lead animator.

Providing voices for primary characters are Jessica DiCicco as Wilhelmina, Bill Fagerbakke as the Scarecrow, Jess Harnell as the Cowardly Lion, JP Karliak as the Tin Man, Kari Wahlgren as Dorothy and Ozma, Laraine Newman as the Wicked Witch, and Steve Blum as Frank.

Other characters that pop in and out of the series include the Patchwork Girl, Woozy, The Hungry Tiger, and Tik-Tok.

Following the MGM movie model, Dorothy wears ruby slippers in the show, and in one episode, The Lollipop Guild is featured.

The storyline in the series has Queen Ozma bestowing onto Dorothy the title of Princess of Emerald City. Dorothy faces her duty with bravery and back-home Kansas feistiness.

Her adversary, Wilhelmina, is the niece of the Wicked Witch of the West, and a practitioner of witchcraft.

It isn't until the second season in the series that The Wizard appears. Upon his return, he works to become a real wizard with actual powers. In his thirst for power, he sets forth to release the spirit of the Wicked Witch, held inside a crystal ball, in hope that the act of kindness will result in a reward of authentic powers. But it is Dorothy who unwitting resurrects the evil witch, placing Oz in danger.

The series features appealing and colorful designs, both in character and background. There's a lot of emphasis on magic, potions, spells, mind-control and supernatural fodder. Add to that a fair dose of humor to the sometimes dark situations, and awkward personal predicaments involving the Scarecrow, Tin Man, and Lion, and you have an entertaining adventure.

The series has enjoyed three seasons since

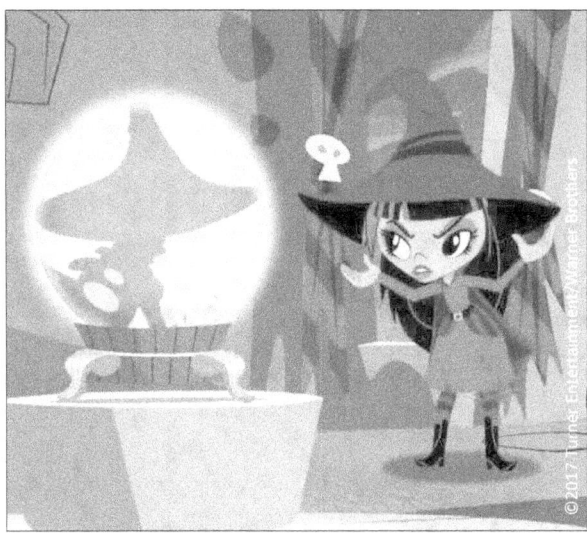

Wilhelmina in *Dorothy and The Wizard of Oz*.

its debut and continues production.

In March 2018, Warner Entertainment released a DVD featuring the first five episodes in the series.

Dorothy and The Wizard of Oz Episode Guide

Beware the Woozy / Magical Mandolin / Toto Unleashed / Official Ozian Exam / Locket Locket in My Pocket / Mixed-up Mixer / Ojo the Unlucky / The Lion's Share / Rules of Attraction / Brain Power of Love / Jinxed / Rise of the Nome King / One-Winged Wally / Wand-erful / No Sleep Sleepover / Lion Catches a Bug / Tik Tok and Tin Man / If I Only Had Some Brawn / The Beast Royales / Time After Time / Kitten Around / Castle Sitters / Stuck on You / Family Matters / The Emerald of Zog / Cooking Up Some Magic / Copy Cat / Snow Place Like Home / Mirror Madness / Everything Coming Up Poppies / Halloween Heist / A Cut Above the Rest / Abraca-Oops / Wheelers of Fortune / Sister Sister / Moody Magic / If the Shoe Fits / Get Smart / Mission Imp-Possible / The Wizard, The Witch and the Crystal Ball / Tin Man and Lion in Wonderland.

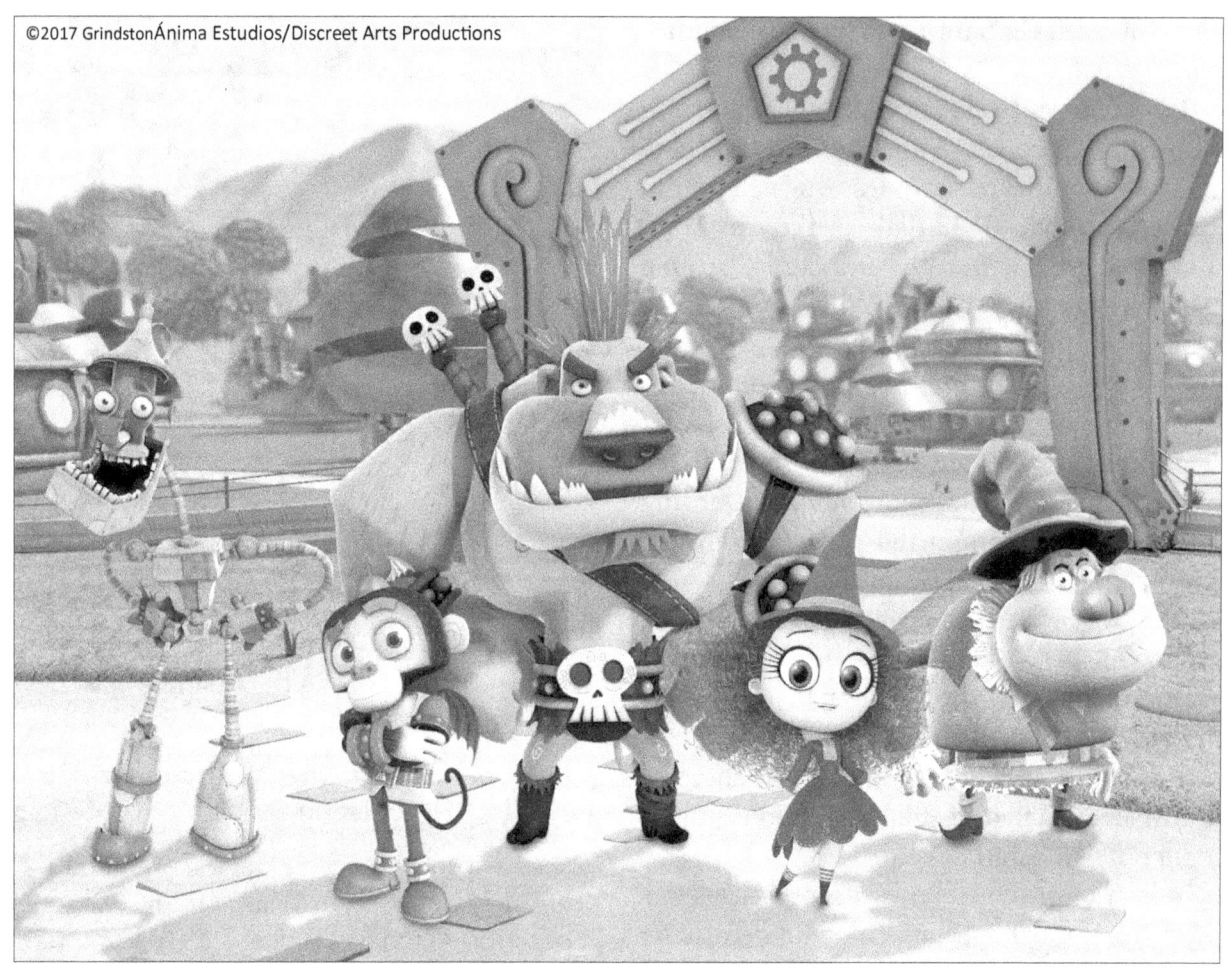

Ánima Estudios/Discreet Arts Productions' *Guardians of Oz*, released in 2015.

CGI Oz Productions (2007-present)

Computer generated imagery has played a role in the Oz realm for over a decade, as of this writing. The first popular use of CGI featuring an adaptation of Lyman Frank Baum's wondrous world came in 2007, with *VeggieTales: The Wonderful Wizard of Ha's*.

The adventure was produced by Big Idea Productions and Arc Productions, with the DVD release by Warner Brothers.

The 49-minute Oz escapade was the 31st episode in the *VeggieTales* Christian children's direct-to-video series. It was produced by Chris Wall and Brian Miller, written by Phil Vischer, and directed by Brian Roberts. Creation of the video facilitated the regular staff of designers, artists, and animators on the series.

In the story, Darby (Junior Asparagus) is the son of a Kansas farmer. Darby learns of a magical amusement park, the Wonderful Land of Ha's, and runs away with his dog Tutu to the destination. Along the way he gathers companions, the Scarecrow (Mr. Lunt), a Tin Man (Larry Cucumber), and a Lion (Pa Grape.)

They meet the Wizard, and discover the

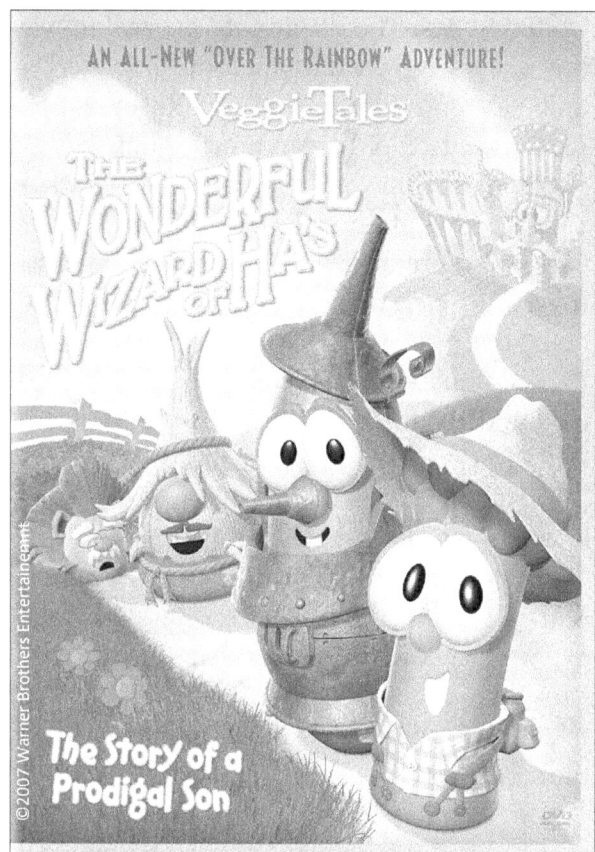

VeggieTales' *The Wonderful Wizard of Ha's*, 2007.

park isn't a fun place to be, after all. There's no place like home isn't just a slogan!

Animation Master Films released two CGI Oz features, *The Tin Woodman of Oz* (2009), and *The Scarecrow of Oz* (2011). Both were released direct to DVD.

The result offers interesting computer imaging, with various results. Some characters appear dark, sharp and creepy, while others are more gentle and soft.

The Tin Woodman of Oz, produced by Martin Hash, was written by Hash, Sydney Cuthbert, Peter Shafer, and Robert Taylor. Twelve individuals directed. The production is the first CB-animated feature produced entirely as an internet collaboration. It runs 90 minutes.

Providing the voices of primary characters were Rhett Jackson, Robert Holmen, David Chase, Teresa Nord, and Nancy Gormezano, among others.

The story takes place after Dorothy has returned to Kansas. The Tin Man and the Scarecrow, appearing as a little boy named Woot, go in search of the metal man's first love, a beautiful girl named Nimmie Aimee.

Over 100 artists, designers and animators from around the world contributed to the creation of *The Tin Woodman of Oz*.

The Animation Master Films sequel, *The Scarecrow of Oz*, retains much of the design as the first, but is a little darker, and gloomy in presentation.

The movie was produced and written by Martin Hash. Holmes Bryant, Nancy Gormezano, Robert Kelly and Mark Skodacek served as art directors. It runs 64-

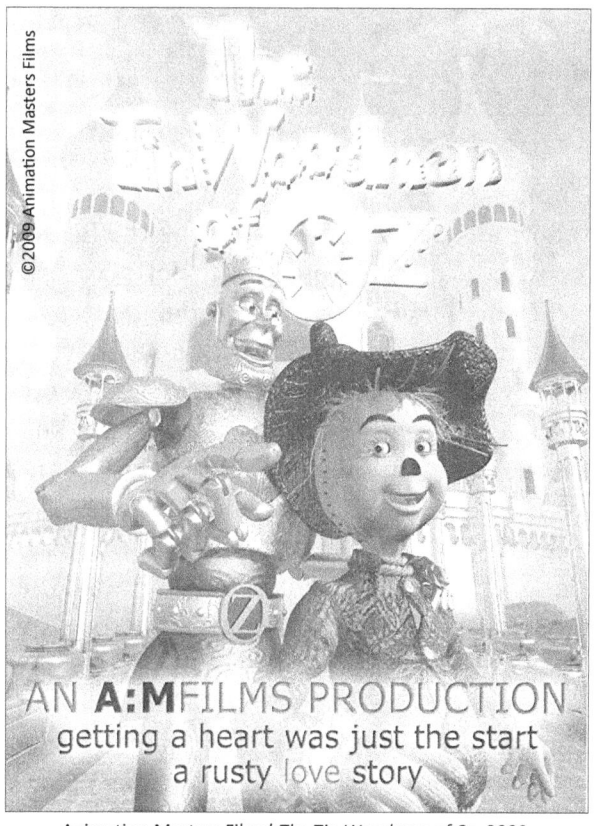

Animation Masters Films' *The Tin Woodman of Oz*, 2009.

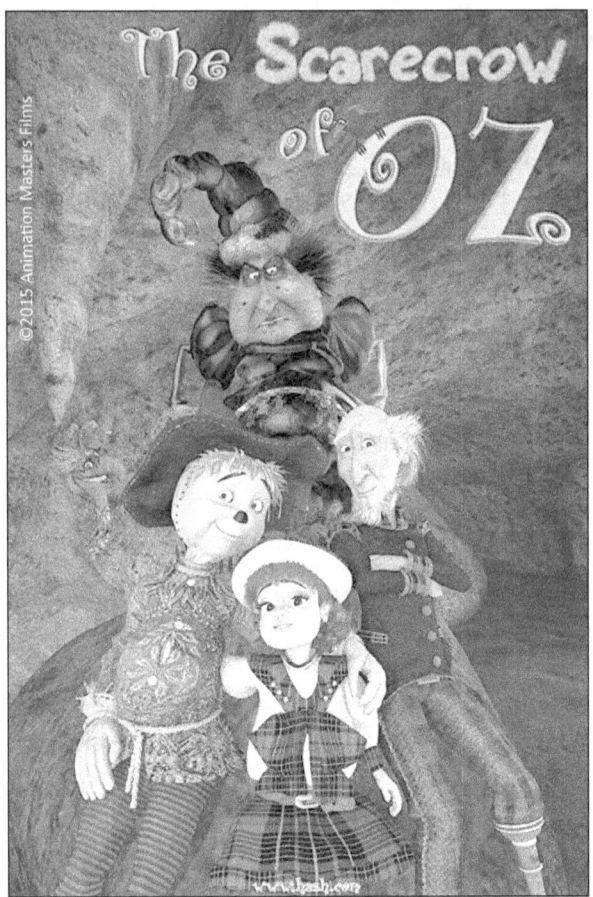

Animation Masters Films' *The Scarecrow of Oz*, 2011.

minutes.

In the story, Cap'n Bill recruits the Scarecrow to help him locate Trot to her new residence in Jinxland. However, trouble lurks as evil King Krewl has taken over the territory.

Providing primary character voices were Holmes Bryant, Nancy Gormezano, Ken Heslip, and four members of the Hash family: Heath, James, Heather, and James.

Like AMF's first endeavor over 100 artists, designers, and animators from around the world contributed to the creation of *The Scarecrow of Oz*.

Legends of Oz: Dorothy's Return is an American-Indian 3D computer animated feature film, produced by Summertime Entertainment, and released May 9, 2014, in the United States. The 88-minute musical movie was a loosely based adaptation of Roger S. Baum's book *Dorothy of Oz*. Roger is the great-grandson of Lyman Frank Baum.

While the film was highly stimulating visually, it brought in only $19 million worldwide, nowhere near the $70 production cost. It was reported to be the only U.S. box office bomb of 2014.

The animated feature was produced by Roland and Ryan Carroll, with Bonne Radford. Will Finn and Dan St. Pierre directed.

The feature boasted the voices of many celebrities and actors, such as Patrick Stewart, Jim Belushi, Dan Aykroyd, Kelsey Grammer, Martin Short and Bernadette Peters, to name a few. Lea Michele performed the voice of Dorothy.

Randi Barnes and Adam Balsam penned the screenplay.

The movie presented 13 original songs, with Toby Chu overseeing music production.

Nearly 200 talented individuals worked on the feature as designers, animators, and visual effects artists.

The story has Dorothy returning to Oz to save her friends the Scarecrow, Tin Man, Cowardly Lion and Glinda from an evil villain known as The Jester.

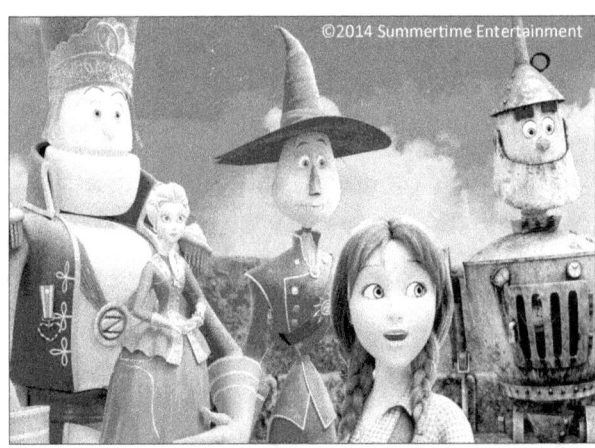

Summertime Entertainment's *Legends of Oz: Dorothy Returns*.

Dorothy is joined by Wiser the Owl, Marshal Mallow, China Princess, and Tugg the boat, in her mission to restore peace to the Emerald City and free it from The Jester's dysfunctional grip.

The movie was released on DVD and Blu-ray by 20th Century Fox Entertainment on August 26, 2014.

Guardians of Oz is a Mexican-Indian 3D computer animated feature film produced by Ánima Estudios/Discreet Arts Productions and released April 10, 2015. The 87-minute movie presented a story not based on any Oz book, per se, and introduced several new characters.

The movie also was released with the title *Wicked Flying Monkeys*.

It was released direct-to-video on DVD in 2017, by Grindstone Entertainment and Lionsgate in the United States. The English version features the voices of Mikey Bolts, Ambyr Childers, and Jenn McAllister, to name a few.

The film, produced by Jose C. Garcia de Letona, Fernando de Fuentes, and Jorge Gutierrez, was directed by Alberto Mar.

The story was written by Gutierrez, Doug Longdale, and Evan Gore.

Gutierrez and his wife, Sandra Equihua, also designed the characters in the film. Venkat Dileep served as the animation production coordinator. Over 120 artists, animators, and special effects technicians worked on the project.

The story takes place after the Wicked Witch of the West has melted away and Dorothy has returned home to Kansas. Glinda presents the Tin Man, Lion, and Scarecrow with the remains of the evil witch's broom, making them the three rulers of Oz.

Evilene, the resurrected Wicked Witch,

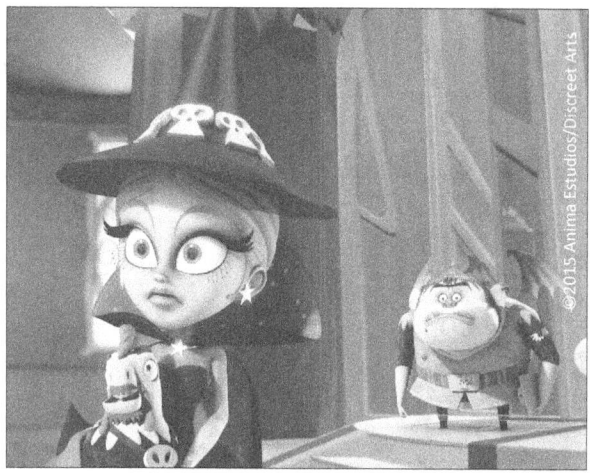

A scene from *Guardians of Oz*.

plots to take back her broom and become the kingdom's ruler. She casts a spell on the trio of rulers, causing disharmony, and leading to the Lion smashing the Tin Man to pieces.

Evilene assumes the throne at the Emerald City. The Lion, Scarecrow, and friends Ozzy and Gaby, take the metal man to the Library of Oz, where he is reassembled.

Ozzy, a friendly winged monkey who hasn't mastered flight and who broke ties with the witch, helps the trio overcome the evil spell. He persuades the other winged monkeys to do good, and join their crusade to destroy Evilene.

In the end, the monkeys rebel and the Wicked Witch is melted for good.

The movie is very good, but also very creepy in design and presentation.

Lost in Oz, a CGI-animated television series produced by Flaunt Productions and Amazon Studios, made its streaming debut on June 26, 2015.

Nineteen talented individuals have served as producers of the episodes in this series created by Abram Makowka, and Darin and Jared Mark.

Serving as primary writers of the series are Makowka, the Marks, and Shion Takeuchi.

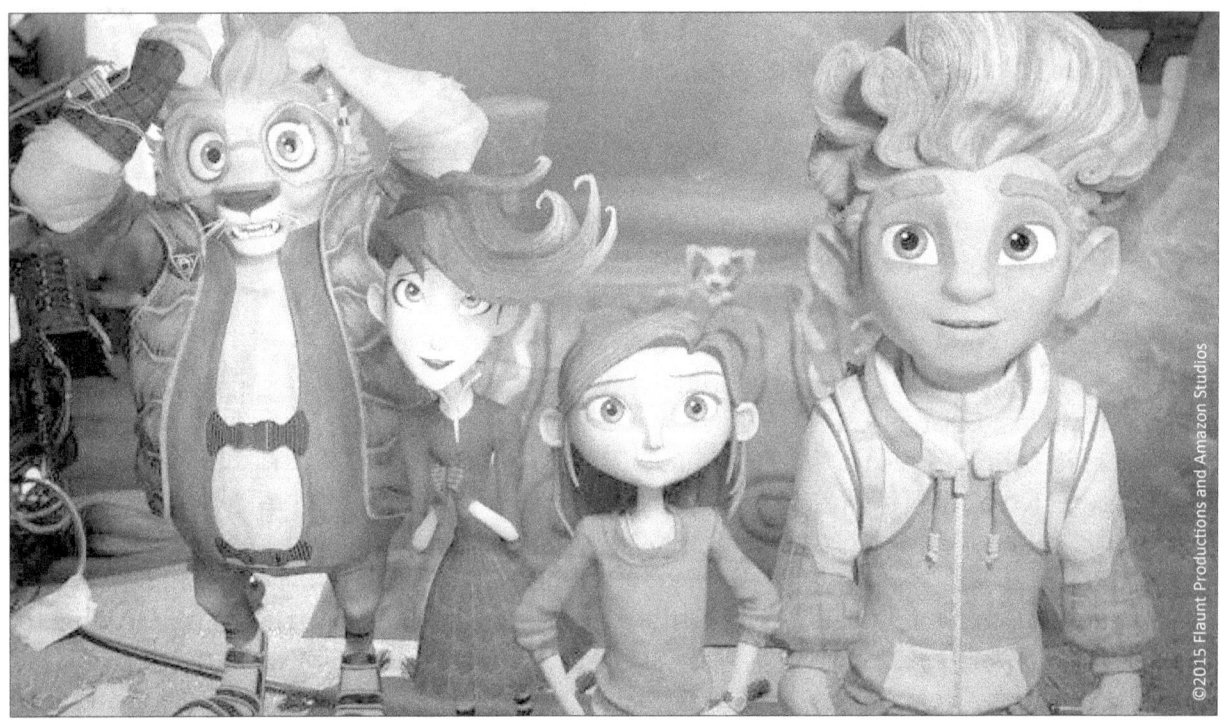

A scene from *Lost in Oz*, produced by Flaunt Productions and Amazon Studios, 2015-present.

Animators, designers, and other production staff number nearly 150.

The series has enjoyed wild popularity in the age of streaming TV, ranking up two seasons with a over a dozen 24-minute episodes.

Performing voices for primary characters in the series are Ashley Boettcher as Dorothy, Jorge Diaz as Ojo, Nika Futterman as West and Chris Cox as the Patchwork Doll.

The animation is well done, and design artistically appealing. There's also real stories. Adventures include such interesting characters as Fitz the Crooked Magician, creatures known as the Growleywogs, and predicaments such as sailing the open sea, and cavernous pits of lava.

The series is available to watch on Amazon streaming video. Amazon Prime members can watch it as part of their subscription.

Lost in Oz Episode Guide

Pilot / Dorothy Meets the Lion / Monkeys Fly / Dorothy Meets the Scarecrow / The Pearl of Pingaree / Wake Up, Wake Up, Wake Up! / Little Black Lies / The Sticks / Down the Yellow Brick Line / Bogspeed, Little Shanks! / 11:11 / Welcome Back, Glinda / Go for Kansas / The Deadly Desert / Magic for Nothing / The Still Season / Villa Roquat / The Magic Cap / Shortcut to Emerald City / Going Forth / Kansas Magic / The Eclipse / Saving Cyra / The Nome King's Belt / Escape from the Nome King / We Speak Mirror.

www.ingramcontent.com/pod-product-compliance
Lightning Source LLC
Chambersburg PA
CBHW062337220526
45469CB00008B/2747